Battlegrou

GERMAN O

CHANNEL
ISLANDS

JERSEY, GUERNSEY, ALDERNEY, SARK

Other guides in the Battleground Europe Series:

Walking the Salient *by* Paul Reed
Ypres - Sanctuary Wood and Hooge *by* Nigel Cave
Ypres - Hill 60 *by* Nigel Cave
Ypres - Messines Ridge *by* Peter Oldham
Ypres - Polygon Wood *by* Nigel Cave
Ypres - Passchendaele *by* Nigel Cave
Ypres - Airfields and Airmen *by* Michael O'Connor
Ypres - St Julien *by* Graham Keech

Walking the Somme *by* Paul Reed
Somme - Gommecourt *by* Nigel Cave
Somme - Serre *by* Jack Horsfall & Nigel Cave
Somme - Beaumont Hamel *by* Nigel Cave
Somme - Thiepval *by* Michael Stedman
Somme - La Boisselle *by* Michael Stedman
Somme - Fricourt *by* Michael Stedman
Somme - Carnoy-Montauban *by* Graham Maddocks
Somme - Pozieres *by* Graham Keech
Somme - Courcelette *by* Paul Reed
Somme - Boom Ravine *by* Trevor Pidgeon
Somme - Mametz Wood *by* Michael Renshaw
Somme - Delville Wood *by* Nigel Cave
Somme - Advance to Victory (North) 1918 *by* Michael Stedman
Somme - Flers *by* Trevor Pidgeon
Somme - Bazentin Ridge *by* Edward Hancock and Nigel Cave
Somme - Combles *by* Paul Reed

Arras - Vimy Ridge *by* Nigel Cave
Arras - Gavrelle *by* Trevor Tasker and Kyle Tallett
Arras - Bullecourt *by* Graham Keech
Arras - Monchy le Preux *by* Colin Fox

Hindenburg Line *by* Peter Oldham
Hindenburg Line Epehy *by* Bill Mitchinson
Hindenburg Line Riqueval *by* Bill Mitchinson
Hindenburg Line Villers-Plouich *by* Bill Mitchinson
Hindenburg Line - Cambrai *by* Jack Horsfall & Nigel Cave
Hindenburg Line - Saint Quentin *by* Helen McPhail and Philip Guest

La Bassée - Neuve Chapelle *by* Geoffrey Bridger
Mons *by* Jack Horsfall and Nigel Cave
Accrington Pals Trail *by* William Turner

Poets at War: Wilfred Owen *by* Helen McPhail and Philip Guest
Poets at War: Edmund Blunden *by* Helen McPhail and Philip Guest
Poets at War: Graves & Sassoon *by* Helen McPhail and Philip Guest

Gallipoli *by* Nigel Steel
Italy - Asiago *by* Francis Mackay

Boer War - The Relief of Ladysmith *by* Lewis Childs
Boer War - The Siege of Ladysmith *by* Lewis Childs
Boer War - Kimberley *by* Lewis Childs
Isandlwana *by* Ian Knight and Ian Castle
Rorkes Drift *by* Ian Knight and Ian Castle

Wars of the Roses - **Wakefield/ Towton** *by* Philip A. Haigh
English Civil War - **Naseby** *by* Martin Marix Evans, Peter Burton and Michael Westaway
Napoleonic - Hougoumont *by* Julian Paget and Derek Saunders

WW2 Pegasus Bridge/Merville Battery *by* Carl Shilleto
WW2 Utah Beach *by* Carl Shilleto
WW2 Gold Beach *by* Christopher Dunphie & Garry Johnson
WW2 Normandy - Jig Beach *by* Tim Saunders
WW2 Omaha Beach *by* Tim Saunders
WW2 Sword Beach *by* Tim Kilvert-Jones
WW2 Battle of the Bulge - St Vith *by* Michael Tolhurst
WW2 Battle of the Bulge - Bastogne *by* Michael Tolhurst
WW2 Dunkirk *by* Patrick Wilson
WW2 Calais *by* Jon Cooksey
WW2 Das Reich – Drive to Normandy *by* Philip Vickers
WW2 Hill 112 *by* Tim Saunders
WW2 Market Garden - Nijmegen *by* Tim Saunders
WW2 Market Garden - Hell's Highway *by* Tim Saunders
WW2 Market Garden - Arnhem *by* Frank Steer
WW2 Channel Islands *by* George Forty

Battleground Europe Series guides under contract for future release:
Somme - High Wood *by* Terry Carter
Somme - German Advance 1918 *by* Michael Stedman
Somme - Beaucourt *by* Michael Renshaw
Walking Arras *by* Paul Reed
WW2 Boulogne *by* Jon Cooksey
WW2 Market Garden - The Island *by* Tim Saunders

Battleground Europe
GERMAN OCCUPATION

CHANNEL ISLANDS

JERSEY, GUERNSEY, ALDERNEY, SARK

George Forty

LEO COOPER

Published by
LEO COOPER
an imprint of
Pen & Sword Books Limited
47 Church Street, Barnsley, South Yorkshire S70 2AS
Copyright © George Forty 2002

ISBN 0 85052 858 5

A CIP record of this book is available
from the British Library

Printed in the United Kingdom by
CPI UK

For up-to-date information on other titles produced under the Leo Cooper
imprint, please telephone or write to:

Pen & Sword Books Ltd, FREEPOST SF5, 47 Church Street
Barnsley, South Yorkshire S70 2BR
Telephone 01226 734555

Opposite: Down with the Union Jack and up with the Swastika! German troops are seen here in early July 1940, about to raise the German flag on the flagpole at Government House, Jersey. It will remain flying there until May 1945. Société Jersiaise

CONTENTS

INTRODUCTION

1940 was a disastrous year for Great Britain and its Allies in the war against Nazi Germany. Everywhere Hitler's all-conquering forces were in the ascendancy, their new Blitzkrieg tactics spreading alarm and despondency, as country after country was overrun, to become part of the 'Greater German Empire'. Then, at the height of summer, France capitulated and Great Britain, now facing the Germans alone, woul only be saved from invasion by the bravery of a handful of RAF pilots. Whilst the air war continued, further German efforts to mount Operation Sealion, the amphibious assault against mainland Great Britain were averted and Hitler forced to change his tactics. Instead he would try to starve out the British, by cutting off their overseas supply lines. However, he would be thwarted in this by the men of the Royal Navy and Merchant Navy, who still controlled the sealanes between the UK and the British Empire, together with those to the neutral, but ever sympathetic, United States of America.

It was a difficult and dangerous time for everyone, especially for the inhabitants of a virtually undefended small group of islands just off the NW coast of France, whose very location appeared to offer the Germans a 'stepping-stone' in the invasion of Great Britain. Operation Sealion might never materialise, but the capture of the Channel Islands would take place and their fiercely independent populations would become the only part of the British Isles to come directly under the heel of the Nazi jackboot. Indeed Hitler would personally become quite mesmerised with the islands, initially seeing them as a postwar holiday health resort, then as an integral and vitally important part of his much vaunted ATLANTIC WALL defences. This would lead not only to the building there of some of the largest and most important defence works and gun positions – Alderney, for example, being described as being a 'concrete battleship' – but also to the garrisoning of the Islands by the largest infantry division in the German Army. While the fighting ability of these troops was never put to the test, their presence on the islands represented both a formidable threat to the Allies and a source of considerable friction within the higher echelons of the German High Command. Many senior generals,

Barbed wire over beauty. Ugly coils of barbed wire despoil this tranquil harbour scene. IWM HU 29113

Generalfeldmarschall Erwin Rommel being one of the most vociferous, complained that this enormous number of men should be made available to defend mainland France, but Hitler refused to change his mind, so convinced was he that their presence in the Channel Islands was an essential part of his defence strategy.

Apart from some relatively minor exchanges of gunfire with passing ships and aircraft, the garrison had just a few engagements with small parties of British commandos, who landed on various islands during the wartime years, to keep them on their toes, so the maintenance of high morale must have been a constant problem. The effect of these commando raids upon Adolf Hitler was way out of proportion to their actual success, infuriating him and constantly reinforcing his determination to keep up the size of the garrison and to improve its defences, so these 'pinpricks' undoubtedly did an excellent job.

Fortunately, the tide of war passed by the Channel Islands without doing much damage, leaving both the islanders and the garrison islolated and very hungry. The Red Cross would partly alleviate some of these problems and the garrision would 'sit out' the rest of the war, ending up to a man in Allied prisoner of war camps, thus fulfilling their destiny – which in the eyes of the rest of the German Army had always been the inevitable end of the 'Canada' Division – so called as they appeared inevitably to be headed for Canadian POW camps! Of course, whilst this was true of the final units, the majority of the actual troops who served there had already been replaced by lower grade, less fit men. It was estimated, for example, that by the summer of 1944, only 30% of the original content 319.ID were still serving on the Islands, the rest having gone East. And of course, the original invaders, 216.ID, had long since departed, to be decimated on the Russian front.

This then is the story of those momentous war years for the Channel Islands and I must thank all the many contacts I have made in these beautiful islands for their help and support. I made most of them initially some years ago, when I was researching for a book for IAN ALLAN PUBLISHING about the life of the German forces on the islands (see Bibliography for details). In particular my grateful thanks must again go to: the Channel Islands Occupation Society, Jersey and Guernsey Branches, especially to their Secretaries, Michael Ginns, MBE and Maj (Retd) Evan Ozanne; the Société Jersiaise (Julia Coutanche); Direct Input Ltd (Peter Tabb); The Alderney Society and Museum (Peter Arnold); The Guernsey Museums Services (Brian Owen); Tomahawk Films (Brian Matthews); Jersey Tourism (Douglas Creedon); States of Guernsey Tourist Board (Louise Cain); Phillimore & Co Ltd (Noel Osborne); The Department of Sound Archives Imperial War Museum; Imperial War Museum Dept of Photography; *The Jersey Evening Post* and *The Guernsey Evening Press*; Howard B Baker, Mr and and Mrs J Brannam, Alec Forty, Michael Payne, Martin Pocock, Hans-Gerhard Sandmann, Maj Phillip Ventham, Werner Wagenknecht and everyone else who has helped me.

Maps – The maps of Alderney are taken from *Alderney: Fortress Island* by T X F Pantcheff and are reproduced here by kind permission of Phillimore and Co Ltd, Shopwyke Manor Barn, Chichester, West Sussex. The map of Jersey is reproduced

The conquerors show their strength. 'Showing the flag' marches through the main ports, etc, took place regularly in Jersey and Guernsey, as the Germans attempted to impose their will on the Islanders. This march took place through St Peter Port, Guernsey in July 1940. Guernsey Museum

Festung Guernsey and **Festung Jersey** were first class records of the occupation produced by the Germans, using their best artists and most skilled photographers. The former were from the Divisional Cartographic Section (**Divisionskartenestelle**) working on behalf of the German CinC of the Channel Islands, Genlt Graf von Schmettow. Here are examples of the drawings: 'Westberg' is an artist's impression of the L'Angle Direction Finding Tower which is still complete, whilst the other drawing prefixed the section on anti-aircraft artillery. Guernsey Museum

by kind permission of Howard B Baker, whilst the map of Guernsey is reproduced by kind permission of Colin Partridge.

Photographs – Reproduction rights for all photographs are as per their respective captions. I must, however, especially thank Michael Ginns, Alec Forty and Martin Pocock for their kind assistance in taking the modern day photographs on Guernsey and Alderney; also Hawksworth Graphics & Print Ltd and Jersey CIOS for those of Jersey. Once again I have also used many of the photographs taken by the late Gerhard Sandmann, thanks to his son Hans-Gerhard.

GEORGE FORTY
Bryantspuddle, Dorset
September 2001

CHAPTER ONE

HOW WE MARCHED!

'After all, what is the road there for but for marching – and how we marched! Day after day in the sun and dust. Forty-five miles was our longest day's march.' That is the opening paragraph of a report[1] written by a German infantry officer, Major Dr Albrecht Lanz, who although he was only a battalion commander in 216 Infantry Division, was destined to become the first military governor of Guernsey, the first British soil to be occupied by the Nazis during World War Two. His battalion had forced marched from Lys in Belgium, via Caen, to the Channel coast around Cherbourg and was now occupying this beautiful area with, as he puts it: 'its shimmering white bays, where the water, crystal-clear and the snow-white sand invited us to bathe. Every company commander was King in his own Kingdom. As the well-to-do inhabitants everywhere had fled, quartering caused no difficulty. In a very short time men and horses were provided for in the best of style, and the alloted task

How we marched! This photograph shows men of the 216. ID, who would be the first German soldiers into the Channel Islands, during their all-conquering march through Europe. H. G. Sandmann

After leaving Duisburg on 9 May, they went on through Belgium and France, reaching the Normandy coast at Laurent-sur-Mer on 25 June. As the photos show, despite the tactics of the Blitzkrieg, the majority of the German infantry still marched, whilst their artillery and supply trains were horsedrawn.

The young, fit and well-trained landser (infantryman) marched and fought their way across the Low Countries, crossing into France and finally marching down the Seine valley, on though the bocage with its high hedgerows, until they reached the sea. All photos were taken by Gerhard Sandmann, late father of Hans-Gerhard Sandmann

– securing the coast – surveyed in all directions and carried out with soldierly thoroughness.'

The leading infantry would soon be followed by more and more German servicemen – soldiers, sailors and airmen, as the *Wehrmacht* tightened its grip on defeated France. Adolf Hitler met a French delegation at Compiègne on 21st June, to accept their surrender, deliberately chosing the same railway carriage in which the Versailles treaty had been signed on 11th November 1918. It had been a remarkable few short weeks since he had launched his *Blitzkrieg* (Lightning War) on the West on 10th May, swiftly overrunning Holland, Belgium and France and forcing the battered British Expeditionary Force and remnants of the other Allied armies, back over the beaches and into the Channel, where they would have perished but for the remarkable heroism of the Royal Navy, ably supported by the 'Little Ships'. The Battle of Britain was yet to be fought and it must have appeared to the victorious Germans that nothing could prevent them from, as they put it: 'Fahren gegen England!' (Marching against England!). And although such dreams of conquest were still 'pie in the sky' for most German servicemen, they would soon become a reality for a small number, amongst whom Albrecht Lanz's men would play a significant part. However, before dealing with the German invasion, we must look first at the reasons why it was so simple and easy to achieve.

When the German occupation forces did arrive in the Channel Islands it would be the very first time that an invader had landed on any part of these beautiful and tranquil islands since 1461, when Jean de Carbonnel, commanding an expeditionary force sent by the Grand Seneschal of Normandy, had captured Mont Orgueil Castle on Jersey. For the next seven years the island was under French rule, until the English retook it in 1468. Since that date the islands had remained as dependencies under the British Crown, although never strictly part of the United Kingdom. Both the main islands of Jersey and Guernsey had Lieutenant Governors (senior serving British Army officers) and Bailiffs (Chief Justices) who were appointed by the Crown.The Bailiffs were the link between the islands administrative bodies and the Lieutenant Governors. At the start of the Second World War, the population of the islands was under 100,000, with roughly 50,000 on Jersey, 40,000 on

Two of the 'little ships', loaded with BEF on their way to England and safety. Author's Collection

Guernsey, 1,500 on Alderney and just 600 on Sark, the majority of whom were born and bred islanders. There were also some expatriate British, some itinerant workers from Ireland and the continent, plus a few Jews although most of the small Jewish community had already moved to England. The mild climate and delightful scenery undoubtedly made the Channel Islands a perfect place to live. Adolf Hitler thought much the same, indeed he went so far as to say that after the war was over and Germany had won, the islands would be handed over to Robert Ley, Head of the German Labour Front, because: '... with their wonderful climate, they constitute a marvellous health resort for the Strength through Joy organisation. The islands are full of hotels as it is, so very little construction would be needed to turn them into ideal rest centres.'[2]

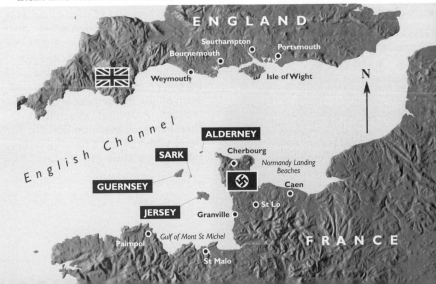

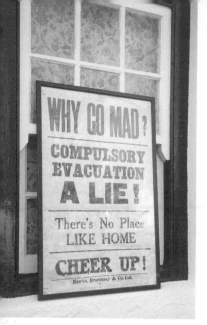

Public notice about evacuation – designed to calm the population. It is now on show in the Occupation Museum, Guernsey. (Brian Matthews)

Muddle and Indecision.

At the start of the war there were no clear cut decisions made as to how the islands would be guarded. Acting on their own initiative, the two Lieutenant Governors had immediately ordered the call-up of their island militias, a decision that was eventually approved by both the War Office and the Home Office. The passing by Parliament in London of the National Service (Armed Forces) Act naturally affected the young men on the islands, who, as they had done at the start of the Great War, had swiftly volunteered in considerable numbers, to serve in the armed forces of Great Britain. The general effect of this in the early months of the war, was a gradual depletion of manpower from the islands, thus seriously weakening the militia. At the same time, the Lieutenant Governors had continually asked for anti-aircraft and coastal defence artillery – plus the skilled manpower to man them – but received little positive help from the 'mandarins' of Whitehall. Indeed, at that time the view of the War Office was that the likelihood of an attack on the Channel

Mr F G French, the Judge (Chief Adminstrator) of Alderney was faced with the problem of what to do with his small island's population, which at that time was just over 1,000. He decided upon evacuation and his decision was supported by the majority – especially after they had seen all the military depart with their families. An orderly evacuation therefore took place on Sunday, 23rd June, when all but a handful were taken off by ship. IWM – HU25940

16

I HAVE APPEALED TO ADMIRALTY FOR A SHIP
TO EVACUATE US.
IF THE SHIP DOES NOT COME, IT MEANS
WE ARE CONSIDERED SAFE.
IF THE SHIP COMES, TIME WILL BE LIMITED.
YOU ARE ADVISED TO PACK ONE SUITCASE
FOR EACH PERSON SO AS TO BE READY.
IF YOU HAVE INVALIDS IN YOUR HOUSE
MAKE ARRANGEMENTS IN CONSULTATION
WITH YOUR DOCTOR. ALL POSSIBLE
NOTICE WILL BE GIVEN.
22nd JUNE 1940

The note which was posted some eight days before the Germans arrived.

Islands was remote and therefore, in their opinion, the weapons would be better employed elsewhere. Even at this early stage it was clear that in the general opinion of the British Government, the islands were not worth defending as they had no real strategic value. This apparently cynical approach did, however, have a basis of sound commonsense, as it would clearly have taken a very large garrison to defend the islands against an all-out attack – and there were few enough trained soldiers available to protect the mainland of Great Britain now that the BEF had gone to France and Belgium. Also, and as was abundantly clear from the scale of destruction and chaos which the German invasion had brought upon the civilian population of Poland, such a defensive battle would wreck the infrastructure of the islands and kill many of their inhabitants. Therefore, positive steps were to be taken to demilitarise the Channel Islands and the regular garrison on Guernsey (1st Battalion The Royal Irish Fusiliers) was removed[3], leaving just some training establishments as the only regular troops on the islands.

However, as the Germans swept through France and the Low Countries, views changed. Initially it was decided (at a meeting of the War Cabinet on 12 June) that the islands should be defended and approval was given to send two infantry battalions as quickly as possible to replace the training

Evacuees arrive in England. This bewildered looking mother and her two children (one aged three years, the other just three months) have just arrived in Weymouth, Dorset, after a twenty hour boat trip from the Channel Islands, 23 June 1940.
IWM - HU 24887

establishments that were stationed there. This was rapidly followed by a complete change of heart as it swiftly came home to all concerned that when the Germans controlled the Channel coast – and this would now be in a matter of days or even hours – the islands would then lose what little strategic importance they had and were thus not worth defending. The training establishments would therefore be withdrawn, the local militia ordered to concentrate on security and anti-sabotage, whilst plans were made to destroy any airfield facilities on the islands which could be of use to the enemy. It was further recommended by the Chief of the Imperial General Staff (CIGS) that the Lieutenant Governors be authorised to surrender the islands should the Germans land, so as to prevent unneccessary bloodshed. Although this was the Army view and plans were put into effect to withdraw the troops concerned, there seems to have been a lack of liaison between the three Services. For example, the Admiralty initially said that they were no longer interested in the Islands and agreed with the War Office that the airfield facilities could be destroyed, whereas the Air Ministry desperately wanted them to remain up and running, so as to be available for use in operations to support of the BEF in France. This need was clearly evidenced by the fact that both 17 and 501

Fighter Squadrons of the RAF, moved their Hurricanes to Jersey from Le Mans and Dinard on 18 June. In addition to the needs of operational aircraft, both Jersey and Guernsey Airways (based at Exeter) flew evacuation flights for some 319 civilians between 19-21 June, so the airfields were still a vital necessity.

Demilitarisation.

Then, as if to show that the left hand really didn't know what the right hand was doing, the War Office announced that they would be sending Light Ack Ack guns (40mm Bofors) to defend both Jersey and Guernsey airfields, and that part of an RE construction company would soon be sent to Guernsey to prepare gun positions! Next, the Admiralty, now faced with the desperate needs of evacuating soldiers from France, warned that they might require to use the islands as a staging post for troops escaping from St Malo. Although this did not happen, small boats from Jersey did help in the British evacuation from the French port between 17-19 June 1940. The 'Fog of War' then descended apace, with troops being evacuated, initially from Alderney, then from all the islands and finally it was decided that the Lieutenant Governors would also be withdrawn. All this activity was accompanied by plans to completely demilitarise the entire islands and to allow those civilians who wished to leave, to be evacuated. Initially many residents clamoured to be provided with transport to the UK, but once the initial panic had subsided, the majority decided to brave it out. Whilst all these plans were being put into effect one vitally important action was unfortunately completely neglected, in that no-one in the British Government appears to have realised that they must inform the enemy that the islands were being demilitarised and would not be defended. However, this might have been done deliberately, so as not to give the enemy any advantage at such a perilous time, but more likely it was just an administrative oversight. As we shall see, this would have serious consquences for some of the unfortunate islanders.

A message from the King.

Nevertheless, the majority of islanders who wished to leave were taken off and arrived safely in the UK, many being taken by sea to Weymouth in Dorset. These included the last of the troops and the militia. The Jersey Militia went en bloc to

MESSAGE FROM THE KING TO THE BAILIFFS OF JERSEY AND GUERNSEY.

For strategic reasons it has been found necessary to withdraw the Armed Forces from the Channel Islands.

I deeply regret this necessity and I wish to assure My people in the Islands that, in taking this decision, My Government has not been unmindful of their position. It is in their interest that this step should be taken in present circumstances.

The long association of the Islands with the Crown and the loyal service the people of the Islands have rendered to my ancestors and Myself are guarantees that the link between us will remain unbroken and I know that My people in the Islands will look forward with the same confidence as I do to the day when the resolute fortitude with which we face our present difficulties will reap the reward of Victory.

The message from King George VI, sent to the Island Baliffs explaining the Government's reasons for withdrawing the British Armed Forces from the Islands.

England where they became the 11th Battalion of the Hampshires, whilst the Guernsey Militia was disbanded, many members then joining the Royal Artillery and the Hampshires. The Lieutenant Governors also departed, having advised the Home Office that the islands were now defenceless. In their turn, on 22nd June, the Home Office drafted the necessary notice to explain the situation, but, as already mentioned, they did not send it out to anyone, as it was considered that the

Germans would immediately mount an invasion. Two days later the Islands Bailiffs received a message from HM King George The Sixth.

As for Major Lanz, an extremely able and intelligent man, who held degrees in both Law and Philsophy, he had spent some of his time liaising the other local German forces and on 29th June, visited the *Kriegsmarine* (Naval) HQ in nearby Cherbourg, where he met *Kaptain-Leutenant* Koch, who had been the last captain of the SS *Hamburg* and had brought his ship with 700 foreign passengers, safely back to its home port two days after the war had begun. During their conversation Lanz had explained that from one of his company positions on the coast at Nez de Joburg, he could see an island, which he had subsequently discovered was Alderney. 'It would be a great thing for us to land over there', he commented and Koch agreed, but explained that the currently there was a lack of suitable shipping.

> 'With this unsatisfied desire in our breasts we parted, not dreaming that the occupation would come about sooner than we thought.'

Two days later, on 2 July, whilst Lanz was having breakfast with his staff in the spacious glass verandah of his luxurious headquarters at Urville, surrounded by subtropical plants, the clatter of a motorcycle engine shattered the calm of the morning. In came a very excited despatch rider with an order that he was to report immediately to the headquarters of the Admiral Commanding Northern France in Cherbourg. Lanz's immediate reaction was that they must have made a mistake as he was Army not Navy and he told the DR that he must have come to the wrong address – what orders could he possibly have from an Admiral? The DR's sunburnt face lit up as he replied with eyes afire:

> 'We're attacking England, sir, the Islands. A rifle company, a troop of heavy machine guns and, if possible, infantry guns of the battalion are to be warned immediately to report to the airport at Cherbourg!'

Not unnaturally Major Lanz, now very excited, was quickly on his way, sitting with his Adjutant in his staff car, tearing along the road to Cherbourg. At the Naval HQ he met by his Divisional Intelligence Officer, Hauptmann Willers, who was acting as divisional liaison officer to the Navy and who introduced him to the German Admiral commanding Northern France, *Vizeadmiral* Eugen Lindau. Together they looked at a map of the islands and discussed the situation. It was explained that the day before (30 June) a Luftwaffe reconnaissance aircraft had landed on Guernsey and had not met any opposition. The High Command had therefore decided that they would take the Channel Islands by a surprise airborne assault, using the naval assault detachment *Gotenhafen*[4] and units of the 216 Infantry Division who were stationed around Cherbourg – 'An exquisite thrill' comments Lanz, 'that it was my battalion that lay nearest to hand.' As the discussion went on it became very clear to Lanz that most of the available information was unreliable and based upon supposition rather than fact. The number of troops needed for the assault seemed to vary between a whole regiment and just a few platoons. Eventually it was agreed that one rifle company reinforced with heavy machine guns, plus the naval assault detchment *Gotenhafen*, would make up the force to be air landed. And, to his great delight, Major Lanz would be in charge: '... Preparation and execution of the plan were entrusted to me,' he comments, with obvious satisfaction.

Thus on one side of the water Major Dr Albrecht Lanz was happily carrying out his planning, somewhat naively thinking that he would be left in peace to execute his plans, despite the ever growing number of senior officers now waiting 'in the wings' all desperate to get into the act. A few miles away the citizens of the object of all his planning waited alone and defenceless, equally naively thinking that their lack of any military muscle would save them from the horrors of war. Clearly there would be some people on both sides who were going to be disappointed.

Notes

1. As quoted from a translation of a report by Major Albrecht Lanz,which appeared in the 1984 *Channel Islands Occupation Review* and appears here with the kind permission of CIOS Guernsey.
2. Taken from *Hitler's Table Talk 1941-44 – His Private Conversations* and attributed to a midday conversation of 22 July 1942. Highly unstable, Robert Ley hanged himself on 25 October 1945, in his cell whilst awaiting trial at Nuremberg.
3. Jersey had lost its garrison infantry battalion fourteen years previously, in 1925.
4. The *Marinestosstruppabteilung 'Gotenhafen'* was one of the units of the Kriegsmarine equivalent to the Royal Marines.

CHAPTER TWO

DENN WIR FAHREN GEGEN ENGLAND!

Armed Reconnaissance

If we are to understand properly the order of events which took place before the Germans were: 'Marching on England!', we must go back to about the 18th June, when air reconnaissance of the Channel Islands had begun by aircraft of Lufflotte 2 (Air Fleet 2), followed later by Luftflotte 3, when they took over responsibility for the support of the operation to occupy the Channel Islands, which was known as Operation *Grüne Pfeil* (Green Arrow). On 20th June, OKW[1], had sent a signal to German Naval Group West saying:

Two of the main players in the unfolding drama were Major Dr Albrecht Lanz (centre of front group), who was the CO of the 2nd Battalion of 216 Infantry Division. He would command the leading troops. With him is Major Dr Maas (right), a fluent English speaker, whom Lanz would use as his interpreter. Guernsey Museum

> *'Occupation of the Channel Islands... is urgent and important. Carry out local reconnaissance and execution thereof.'*

Aerial reconnaissance was therefore carried out with mixed results. On the one hand it was clear that there were no occupied artillery emplacements, no military aircraft on the airfields and not all that much sea traffic. However, there was still quite a lot of activity at the main ports of St Helier on Jersey and St Peter Port on Guernsey, with motor vehicles on the quays and merchant ships visible – but were they bringing in troops, weapons, equipment and ammunition, or were they merely evacuating civilians? The only answer was to fly more reconnaissance missions, but this time to make them more aggressive. Events came to a head on Friday, 28 June 1940, when six Heinkel He 111 medium bombers appeared over the islands, having taken off from an airstrip near Cherbourg, earlier that afternoon. Not only did they fly low over St Helier and St Peter Port, but they dropped some 180 bombs on the islands and machine-gunned both ports, killing a total of 44 civilians and wounding many more. One of those at the receiving end was Mr E J de Ste Croix, who had lived in Jersey since the age of five and had worked as an electrician with the Jersey Electric Company since leaving school. However, as there was very little work once war had been declared, the single men had been asked to find jobs elsewhere. He had done so and now worked for George Troy which was a firm of stevedores at the docks. That afternoon he was working on a ship called the *Hull Trader*, loading barrels of potatoes at the Albert Pier. He had seen German aircraft fly over on a number of occasions, taking photographs, but this was the first time they had taken any aggressive action. He recalled:

> *'On that afternoon , I was working at the Albert Pier ...We were loading potatoes into a small freighter called the* Hull Trader *which was one of the very last ships to leave before the occupation began... I was down in the hold ... they came out of the blue. In fact I don't ever remember the siren going. I don't think it ever did. And they dropped these bombs which landed across the harbour and did extensive damage. We were ordered out of the ship to take shelter on the pier where best we could. I remember at the time, the strange things that men do under stress, where some men had crawled under a tarpaulin. What*

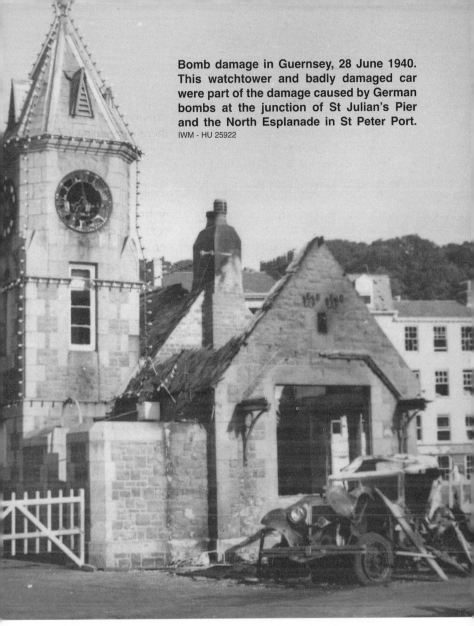

Bomb damage in Guernsey, 28 June 1940. This watchtower and badly damaged car were part of the damage caused by German bombs at the junction of St Julian's Pier and the North Esplanade in St Peter Port.
IWM - HU 25922

shelter they expected to find there, Heaven knows! Others gathered together in groups under the framework of cranes, quite out in the open. But I made a beeline with several other fellows, much older than me of course – probably men among them who had been under fire themselves in the First War – and there used to be in those days almost opposite to where the ship was loading,

25

a little tea shack for the use of the dockers. I remember we jammed ourselves in between the tea shack and the wall of the Albert Pier promenade, where we were comparatively safe. We weren't there awfully long before we came out. And by then the crew were already battening down the hatches and preparing to leave... obviously we were all keen to get back home and make sure our folks were all right and let them know we were OK,

Front page of Guernsey Evening Press

because several people had been killed and wounded as you know.' [2]

It was much the same at St Peter Port, although here there was some retaliation in that the twin AA Lewis guns on the mail steamer *Isle of Sark*, which was embarking passengers for England at the time, opened fire, but none of the planes were damaged. There were casualties from bombing in other parts of the islands as well as in the actual dock areas, whilst the Guernsey lifeboat which had been off Noirmont on its way to Jersey, was machine-gunned, killing one of the crew. Casualties were taken to the General Hospital and a large proportion of the residents of both ports went off to sleep in the countryside that night.

The reason why

Whilst it was obviously the Luftwaffe who were responsible for these casualties, it has to be said that the British Home Office were at least partly responsible in that they deliberately did not release the information that the islands were demilitarised until after the air raid had taken place. Indeed, it wasn't broadcast until the 28th and then deliberately reported in the press to make it look as though the Germans had carried out their raids knowing that the islands were undefended. Officially, it was even worse, in that they did not formally tell the German Government until the 30 July, so the raids should be viewed in that context.

One Jersey citizen commented after the war, in a recording he made for the Imperial War Museum:

'We now know that the Germans were quite mystified after their air raid as to why there was no anti-aircraft fire. They assumed this was a trap to draw them closer in... because nothing had been declared. On that Friday, and I think it is interesting to record this... the air-raid occurred about seven o'clock in the evening , at nine o'clock we heard that the Channel Islands had been declared open and would not be defended. On the eight o'clock news on the Saturday morning – and I hope this doesn't sound anti-British, but it is factually true, at eight o'clock on the Saturday morning of the same new bulletin, we heard about the bombing. Now the reaction in the minds of everyone in the UK must have been: "There you are, they declare a place undefended on the nine o'clock news on the Friday and

here we hear within hours that the place has been bombed and many people killed". But it didn't really happen that way.[3]

Operation Grüne Pfeil

When the original Op *Grüne Pfeil* (Green Arrow) – the operation to capture the Channel Islands – had been first mooted, it had been estimated that a force of at least six battalions would be needed – three for Jersey, two for Guernsey and one for Alderney. However, due to the obvious difficulties which would be encountered getting ashore on the difficult, rocky shores, these battalions would be only lightly equipped. There would also be a naval ground element – a *Marinestosstruppabteilung* of naval assault group – in support, whilst naval bombardment and air strikes from dive bombers would be necessary to precede and support the assault in the usual *Blitzkrieg* fashion. It would also be vital to protect the landing craft (which were in very short supply) from the Royal Navy who were bound to be active, even if the British Army and the RAF were otherwise engaged. However, the lack of retaliation to the raids on the 28th, caused the German High Command to scale down their operations to one battalion for

This Messerschmitt Bf 109E on the airfield at Cherbourg. One of the best single-seat fighters of the war, it was matched by the performance of the British Spitfire and Hurricane.
Hans-Gerhard Sandmann

Jersey, another for Guernsey and just a platoon for Alderney. They would be supported by the *Kriegsmarine Abteilung Gotenhafen* and a *Flak* (light AA) detachment from the *Luftwaffe*, who would also provide constant air support.

An individual initiative

The next event was most certainly not planned and took all those involved in the preparations for Op Green Arrow completely by surprise. A meeting in Paris on 30 June had just decided that another armed aerial reconnaissance would be flown the following day and that an aircraft would be detailed to land at one of the airports to see what reaction there would be, when, just as the meeting was ending, news came through that Luftwaffe pilot, *Hauptmann* Liebe-Pieteritz, whilst on a routine air recce, had landed and taken off again from the Guernsey airfield! He had been leading a flight of Dornier Do 17Ps, the photographic version of that versatile aircraft, and, acting entirely on his own initiative, had landed, whilst his other aircraft circled above giving him protection. Liebe-Pieteritz had entered the airport building and found it empty. His bold sortie was interrupted by the arrival of some RAF Bristol Blenheims and so he had to leave in some haste – dropping his pistol in his rush to get airborne. However, he was able to report to *Airflotte* 3 that the airfield was unmanned, which led to a second landing that evening, when a party of *Luftwaffe* personnel from *Aufklarungsgruppe* 123 (Recce Group123) under a *Hauptmann* von Obernitz, took control of Guernsey airport. Von Obernitz shortly had a visitor, namely the head of the Guernsey police, Inspector William R Schulpher, who brought with him a letter, in English, from the Bailiff (Victor Carey) which read as follows:

> 'This island has been declared an Open Island by His Majesty's Government of the United Kingdom. There are no armed forces of any description. The bearer has been instructed to hand this communication you. He does not understand the German language.'

He then handed over the letter to a Major Hessel, who was in overall command of the German party.

After handing over the note, Inspector Schulpher then drove Major Hessel into St Peter Port to meet the Bailiff. Whilst he was in the town, Hessel also ordered a local milliners shop to make him a German Imperial War Flag, which he intended to fly from the signal mast at the aerodrome terminal. Clearly now the occupation could take place without any form of operational assault, so there need not be any further blooodshed, indeed, there would be a German welcoming party for the leading troops.

Back in Cherbourg the talking was still going on. There was still some doubt expressed as to the actual state of the islands' defences – for example, much was still being made about the artillery positions which had been photographed – little did they realise that these positions were now occupied by some ancient cannons and were well over one hundred years old. Eventually, however, it was agreed that just one single rifle company from Lanz's battalion would be needed, suitably reinforced with heavy machine guns and the *Kriegsmarine* Assault Detachment *Gotenhafen*. Lanz was told that nine Ju52/3m transport aircraft were being allocated to him. These remarkable, ungainly looking aircraft which appeared to have been made from sheets of corrugated iron, were the mainstay of the *Luftwaffe* transport fleet. The aircraft allocated to Op Green Arrow were scheduled to arrive from Paris at the Cherbourg West airfield at Querqueville, at about 0930hrs. 'As this operation was principally a Naval action,' wrote Major Lanz:

'Admiral Lindau proposed to put the Naval assault detachment Gotenhafen in the first Jus. Directly the conference was over we went out to the airfield at which in the meantime the Naval assault detachment Gotenhafen had already arrived. The alloted groups of my battalion rolled up at about the same time, to the Naval Barracks where No 1 Coy, whose positions were near the airfield, were billeted. "Don't let too many people be seen on the airfield" was the order, for only two days before a British plane had disposed of the Admiral Commanding's car, which was on the airfield, diving three times in broad daylight. Quickly various questions were discussed with the Admiral's Chief of Staff. With Oberleutenant Rettinghaus, OC Naval assault detachment Gotenhafen, dispositions and loading were decided, rifles and heavy weapons separated, and an Officer was entrusted with the supervision of the operation after our departure.'

Whilst these preparations were taking place a mass of high ranking officers had descended upon the unfortunate Major

Men of 216 ID get ready to board their Ju 52 at Cherbourg West airfield. Hans-Gerhard Sandmann

Lanz – for example, there were: *Oberstleutnant* Gene, the commanding officer of Lanz's regiment (*infanterie* regiment 396) together with his adjutant, *Oberleutnant* Niebuhr, who was naturally interested in the fact that part of his regiment was on its way to British soil; *Oberstleutenant* Plocher, Chief of Staff of No 5 Air Corps (*Fliegerkorps*) who said that he would definitely be accompanying the landing force, then General der Flieger Hugo Sperrle, who commanded *Luftflotte* 3 There was, however,

View over the Tante Ju's pilot's shoulder as they took off from Cherbourg West airfield. Hans-Gerhard Sandmann

no sign of the promised 'Tante Jus' – as the Ju 52s were affectionately called by one and all. Sperrle, who had commanded the German Condor Legion in Spain during the Civil War, fortunately took charge of the situation. First of all he discovered that the Ju52s had been held up by thick ground mist around Paris and had had to land at a number of other airfields to refuel, which had broken up the formation. He then despatched a Messerchmitt Me110 on a reconnaissance mission over Guernsey, discovering that Major Hessel and his party were still in position at the airfield. Then at long last, the first two Ju 52s arrived, but there was no sign of the other seven. 'We could stay no longer', wrote Major Lanz, after they had waited a further half an hour:

'we decided, after discussing it with OTL Plocher, to set off in these two machines and get the business started at last. Plocher announced his intention of joining us with his machine and a Radio-Ju. Quickly two platoons of the Naval assault detachment Gotenhafen were loaded into the two Jus and already the engines were roaring. With many good wishes from all those left behind, who envied us our glorious task, we rolled to the taking off place. With a drone of engines one Ju followed the other across the field. Soon the ground vanished beneath our feet. A few seconds later the machines turned out to sea in a great loop and arranged themselves in ordered formation. Turning to the land again we crossed Cape Flamanville and out to the open sea, directed towards the islands, the first British territory which German soldiers have trod.

'We had scarcely left the Mainland when there was a slight jolt to the stomach as the Jus dived down towards the foaming waves for we could only fly between 25 and 50 yards above the wave-crests in order to keep out of sight of British fighters and remain hidden. Evenly the engines droned their familiar song, already in the distance the first contours of the longed-for Island began to show themselves. Then someone began to sing and in a moment the whole of the occupants of the aircraft joined in. With steady voice and shining eyes the battle song resounded through the aircraft: "Denn wir fahren gegen England" – "For we're marching against England". Now at last we really were. An unforgettable moment. We still didn't know what to expect, battle or peace. When we approached the coast our Ju climbed and soon we were circling over Guernsey. Quickly the

Good shot of the Junkers Ju 52/3m transport aircraft that carried the assault force. This 'maid of all work', was used all over the world by the Luftwaffe and, despite its strange appearance – it looked as though it was constructed out of sheets of corrugated iron – it was a reliable and much-liked aircraft. IWM - H 8492

experienced eye of the pilot picked out the airfield, one more loop and already the machine was on the runway and halted in front of the airport building. I and my Adjutant were the first to jump out of the plane – I didn't want anyone to take that pleasure from me. Now we had British ground beneath our feet. It was now 1445hrs. Rapidly each platoon received its orders.'

Lanz and the others were met by a smiling Major Hessel, who

Landfall. Their first glimpse of the Channel Islands, as the aircraft approaches land. Hans-Gerhard Sandmann

told them at all was quiet and that there had been no enemy opposition. He also spoke about the flag he had had made in St Peter Port and produced it. Just after 1500 hours the first German Imperial War Flag was hauled up the mast at the airport building and: 'The beautiful isle of Guernsey was thereby visibly taken under German overlordship.' Lanz also comments that a few days later he received a bill from the shop which he would pass on to Major Hessel for him to frame and hang up with the flag in the mess of his Recce Squadron.

The other Jus now started to arrive, and at about 1600 hours the divisional commander of the 216 Infantry Division, *Generaleutenant* Herman Boettcher, landed together with his deputy and adjutant. With them came Admiral Lindau, anxious

Orders of German Comdt Guernsey

ORDERS OF THE COMMANDANT OF THE GERMAN FORCES IN OCCUPATION OF THE ISLAND OF GUERNSEY

(1)—ALL INHABITANTS MUST BE INDOORS BY 11 P.M. AND MUST NOT LEAVE THEIR HOMES BEFORE 6 A.M.

(2)—WE WILL RESPECT THE POPULATION IN GUERNSEY; BUT, SHOULD ANYONE ATTEMPT TO CAUSE THE LEAST TROUBLE, SERIOUS MEASURES WILL BE TAKEN AND THE TOWN WILL BE BOMBED.

(3)—ALL ORDERS GIVEN BY THE MILITARY AUTHORITY ARE TO BE STRICTLY OBEYED.

(4)—ALL SPIRITS MUST BE LOCKED UP IMMEDIATELY, AND NO SPIRITS MAY BE SUPPLIED, OBTAINED OR CONSUMED HENCEFORTH. THIS PROHIBITION DOES NOT APPLY TO STOCKS IN PRIVATE HOUSES.

(5)—NO PERSON SHALL ENTER THE AERODROME AT LA VILLIAZE.

(6)—ALL RIFLES, AIRGUNS, PISTOLS, REVOLVERS, DAGGERS, SPORTING GUNS, AND ALL OTHER WEAPONS WHATSOEVER, EXCEPT SOUVENIRS, MUST, TOGETHER WITH ALL AMMUNITION, BE DELIVERED AT THE ROYAL HOTEL BY 12 NOON TO-DAY, JULY 1.

(7)—ALL BRITISH SAILORS, AIRMEN AND SOLDIERS ON LEAVE IN THIS ISLAND MUST REPORT AT THE POLICE STATION AT 9 A.M. TO-DAY, AND MUST THEN REPORT AT THE ROYAL HOTEL.

(8)—NO BOAT OR VESSEL OF ANY DESCRIPTION, INCLUDING ANY FISHING BOAT, SHALL LEAVE THE HAR-BOURS OR ANY OTHER PLACE WHERE THE SAME IS MOORED, WITHOUT AN ORDER FROM THE MILI-TARY AUTHORITY, TO BE OBTAINED AT THE ROYAL HOTEL. ALL BOATS ARRIVING FROM JERSEY, FROM SARK OR FROM HERM, OR ELSEWHERE, MUST REMAIN IN HARBOUR UNTIL PERMITTED BY THE MILITARY TO LEAVE.

THE CREWS WILL REMAIN ON BOARD. THE MASTER WILL REPORT TO THE HARBOURMASTER, ST. PETER-PORT, AND WILL OBEY HIS INSTRUCTIONS.

(9)—THE SALE OF MOTOR SPIRIT IS PROHIBITED, EXCEPT FOR USE ON ESSENTIAL SERVICES, SUCH AS DOC-TORS' VEHICLES, THE DELIVERY OF FOODSTUFFS, AND SANITARY SERVICES WHERE SUCH VEHICLES ARE IN POSSESSION OF A PERMIT FROM THE MILITARY AUTHORITY TO OBTAIN SUPPLIES.

THESE VEHICLES MUST BE BROUGHT TO THE ROYAL HOTEL BY 12 NOON TO-DAY TO RECEIVE THE NECESSARY PERMISSION.

THE USE OF CARS FOR PRIVATE PURPOSES IS FORBIDDEN.

(10)—THE BLACK-OUT REGULATIONS ALREADY IN FORCE MUST BE OBSERVED AS BEFORE.

(11)—BANKS AND SHOPS WILL BE OPEN AS USUAL.

(Signed) THE GERMAN COMMANDANT OF THE ISLAND OF GUERNSEY

JULY 1, 1940.

not to miss the historic occasion. Major Hessel then formally handed over command of Guernsey to Major Lanz, because Hessel needed to get back to the rest of his squadron who were still in France. However, before he left he and Lanz, presumably again driven by Inspector Schulpher, in one of the many civilian cars which had been abandoned at the airport by civilians on their way to England, went down into St Peter Port. They were also accompanied by Major Dr Maas, the English-speaking Medical Officer of the naval assault detachment *Gotenhafen*, who would become most important to the proceedings as Lanz did not speak much English – Lanz considered Dr Maas to be an exemplary interpreter, who would take on the job of official garrison interpreter and head of public relations.

Their first stop was at the *Royal Hotel* on the Esplanade, in which Hessel had made his temporary HQ (it was never subsequently used as an HQ, but rather became the chosen place for billeting visiting senior officers, whilst its restaurant was a favourite officers dining out spot. The then current manager, a Mr Mentha, was of German extraction , so kept his post and ran the hotel throughout the war years). Outside the Royal a large crowd of civilians had assembled, all anxious to discover what was happening. They had read the first list of German Occupation Regulations which had been published in the previous night's newspaper, but were clearly anxious to know more about what was to happen next.

The next person to be visited was the Bailiff and Lanz explains how they drove to the Bailiff's country residence, rang the bell and were ushered into a 'large richly furnished living room' where they met the Bailiff . For Lanz this was: 'easily the proudest moment of this war.' Victor Carey, whom Lanz describes as being an old gentleman of 68 in a dark suit, bowed deeply before the representatives of the German Army and thanked them for the correct behaviour of the German troops.

'He also promised to make all the necessary arrangements for our wishes and regulations to be carried out in the smallest detail. Everything we needed was at our disposal.'

They then returned to the airport, Hessel departed and Lanz turned his attention on to what should be done to occupy the rest of the Channel Islands. First and foremost there was Jersey, which was some sixteen miles away and almost twice the size of Guernsey. He had no idea what the situation was there and probably feared for the worst. However, he need not have worried as action had already been taken to call upon both Jersey and Alderney to surrender. Admiral Lindau had arranged for a message to be dropped over both islands on the early hours of 1st July, in pouches with white streamers (said to have been made from the bed linen of French officers' sleeping quarters on the airfield in France from whence they were despatched). The message was an ultimatum, from *General der Flieger* Dr Ing Wolfram Feiherr von Richthofen[4], Commander of the *Luftwaffe* in Normandy and addressed (for the one dropped in Jersey) to the Chief of the Military and Civil Authorities, Jersey (St Helier). It read:

'I intend to neutralize military establishments in Jersey by occupation.

As evidence that the island will surrender the military and other establishments without resistance and without destroying them, a large White Cross is to be shown as follows, from 7am July 2nd 1940

a. In the centre of the airport in the East of the Island

b. On the highest point of the fortifications of the port

c. On the square to the north of the Inner Basin of the Harbour

Moreover, all fortifications, buildings, establishments and houses are to show the White Flag.

If these signs of peaceful surrender are not observed by 7am July 2nd, heavy bombardment will take place.

a. Against all military objects

b. Against all establishments and objects useful for defence

The signs of surrender must remain up to the time of the occupation of the Island by German troops.

Representatives of the Authorities must stay at the airport until the Occupation.

All Radio traffic and other communications with Authorities outside the Island will be considered hostile actions and will be followed by Bombardment.

In case a peaceful surrender, the lives, property and liberty of peaceful inhabitants are solemnly guaranteed.

The Commander of the German Air Forces in Normandy
RICHTHOFEN
General'

No reply having been received two aircraft were sent to

discover what was happening. *Leutnant* Richard Kern landed at Jersey airport and to quote from a German newspaper report:

'... lonely and deserted, his machine rolled over the wide, empty field. Then Leutnant Kern gripped his pistol and jumped to the ground. He strode towards the administration building followed by the machine, its machine guns at the ready. Nothing happened. Finally, from the airport building emerged an excited man, who to the astonishment of the newcomers, spoke in German. He took the Lieutenant to the telephone and got in touch with the Bailiff.'

The Bailiff, Mr Alexander Coutanche, explained over the telephone that Jersey was willing to surrender and that the reason why there were no white flags showing was that the States which made up Jersey had only just made their formal decision. He asked Kern to ensure that the German authorities were informed as quickly as possible and Kern promised to do so. He also arranged for a formal meeting to complete the surrender at 6pm that evening, however, he also said that the Islanders should assume that from now on they were under German occupation. Leutnant Kern then flew over to see Major Lanz in Guernsey and explained the situation. 'That was good enough for us' recalled Lanz:

'off we went alone to complete the formal surrender... twenty minutes later we were circling over the airfield on Jersey... as we rolled across the field to the airport building Hauptmann von Obernitz came smiling towards us and reported that he had landed with his men on the Island that day and taken possession of it'.

He also said that everything on Jersey was quiet and under control. Lanz radioed Cherbourg and in a short time the first 'Tante Jus' arrived, carrying his No 1 Company. Major Lanz had borrowed the German Imperial War Flag from Major Hessel before leaving Guernsey – promising his head as security – so that they could hold a proper flag raising ceremony as they had done at Guernsey airport. 'On the right flank was OTL Plocher, with all the other officers present,' wrote Lanz later:

'then a section of the Luftwaffe consisting of the crews of the Obernitz Squadron, then the men of the Naval Assault Detachment Gotenhafen and finishing with the whole of No 1 Company. Kapitanleutanant Koch, who, naturally was with us, had the task of hoisting with his own hands the German Imperial

War Flag high above the roof of the airport building. I myself gave the orders. With arms at the slope and eyes right, over the airfield rang the command: 'Hoist Flag!' Slowly and ceremonially over this British territory also, for the first time in history rose the German Imperial War Flag... Now Jersey too, was under German overlordship.'

After the ceremony, Major Lanz appointed the commander of his No 1 Company, Hauptmann Gusseck, as the first Island Commander of Jersey, gave him a quick briefing and then returned to Guernsey to deal with the endless number of administrative points that had arisen – not the least being the fact that the Royal Hotel, his temporary 'home', was almost without windows, all of which had been blown out by the bombing attack on the 28th. It is interesting to note that Gusseck was no stranger to Jersey, having been a POW there during WWI – in a camp at the foot of Mont a la Brune, St Brelade.

Jersey airport. The Bailiff, Alexander Coutanche and the Attorney-General, Duret-Aubin (far left) talk with Staffel Kapitan von Obernitz. Lt Kern, who was the first German to land in Jersey, looks on. IWM - HU 25961

Sark. Also to receive a visit from Majors Lanz and Maas was the Dame of Sark, Sibyl Hathaway, seen here at La Seigneurie.
IWM - HU 25974

Meeting the Dame of Sark

Major Lanz continued with his hectic schedule and the following day he and Major Maas went by boat to the small island of Sark, where they met Sibyl Hathaway, then Dame of Sark, the island's ruler and a lady of considerable ability and presence. In her autobiography she describes this first meeting, commenting that she thought Lanz was: 'a fair minded man, who would never try to trick anyone by low cunning', but that she did not like Dr Maas, finding him just: 'too smooth!' She goes on to explain how they produced a large poster written in both English and German entitled: 'Orders of the Commandant of the German Forces of the Channel Islands', which dealt with such 'Dos and Donts' as the times of the curfew (2300-0600hrs daily); the handing in of all firearms; the forbidding of liquor sales and the closing of all licensed premises; the forbidding of the assembly of more than five people in the streets at one time, and that no boats could leave the harbour without permission from the military authority. All cameras and wireless sets could be kept for the time being – but must not be used. When she had read the notice carefully, Dame Sybil turned to Lanz and said in German: 'Please sit down. I will see that these orders are obeyed.' The two officers were very surprised and Lanz commented that she did not appear to be the least afraid of them, which gave her the ideal opportunity to innocently remark: 'Is there any reason why I should be afraid of German officers?' The question had the desired effect in that they at once assured her that she had nothing to fear and they immediately became most affable, Lanz even going so far as to tell her that if she ever had any problems she should communicate directly with the Commandant of the Channel Islands. The fair-minded Lanz was not to know that Dame Sibyl would take full advantage of this promise and often go over the head of the local Commandant of Sark (initially this was just an *Obergrefreiter* (Corporal)) which, as she put it: 'put a stop to any petty tyranny by local officers in Sark!' On the 4 of July, a garrison of just ten men under *Obergrefreiter* Obenhauf, became the alloted garrision, and Obenhauf, who had been told by Major Lanz to see the Dame as quickly as possible, was soon on excellent terms with her. Dame Sibyl described the first few months of military control as being: 'quiet and uneventful'.

On to Alderney

The now almost completely deserted island of Alderney would be the next place to be visited by the indefatigable Lanz.

The Royal Hotel on the Esplanade at St Peter Port was used by Lanz as a temporary headquarters, having been commandeered by Maj Hessel. It was minus many of its windows as a result of the air-raid. Hans-Gerhard Sandmann

The island had, some days prior to the surrender, on or about 20 June, been depopulated, ships being sent to remove almost all the inhabitants to Weymouth, Dorset. A handful had also made their own way to Guernsey. Seven elderly couples had flatly refused to go anywhere and had had to be forcibly removed by the Guernsey St John's Ambulance Brigade. Those who remained on Alderney were the family of Frank Oselton, a farmer. He was joined later by George Pope and his family. Pope would become the lighthouse pilot for the Casquets Lighthouse and work throughout the Occupation for the Germans[6] Major Lanz went by air to Alderney, using a Fieseler Fi 156 *Storch* (Stork), the remarkable STOL (Short Take-Off and Landing) aircraft which was used virtually everywhere the German forces operated, needing only a 60m run to take off and landing in about 20m. There was of course no one for Lanz to talk to there, so after a quick look around, Lanz left. Subsequently one of the infantry platoons from his battalion was sent as the initial garrison, under an *Unterfeldwebel* (Sergeant) Schmidt. Initially they had to survive on the food stocks that had been left by the departing residents, until a proper supply system could be organised.

Finally, the tiny islets of Herm and Jethou, which lie between Sark and Guernsey were visited, searched and officially taken over, together with their populations of rabbits, pheasants and seabirds. Especially mentioned were cormorants, oyster catchers and many kinds of diving birds and the fact that, as every cormorant kills its own weight in fish every day, the Germans were asked to arrange to cull them, as all weapons had had to be given up. So as Lanz put it:

'... hunting these nimble divers that swim 100 yards or more under water to escape was a most interesting recreation from all the writing and administrative work in the office'.

Working together

Major Dr Albrecht Lanz closes his reminisences in a most conciliatory way:

'Thus everything fell quickly into its place, both Army and Administration took pains to work together and meet each other half way. The mass of the population gratefully recognised the correctness, generosity and obligingness of the occupying troops. From the many letters that went abroad and so were subject to

41

censorship one could make a very interesting cross-section of existing opinion. A point often repeated was put well by one writer: the German Commandant did more in 48 hours than the States in 48 years. The tempo we had struck up was not customary here.'

We will look in more detail at the relationship between the German garrision and those whom they garrisoned, however, it is perfectly fair to say that undoubtedly the initial German Servicemen were so careful in their dealings with the inhabitants that many people were convinced that they must have been hand-picked. Certainly Lanz was an excellent choice for the job, but perhaps had too romanticised a view of what was happening. For example, he clearly did not realise the true feelings of the fiercely independent islanders. He would die far away from beautiful Guernsey, in the snows of the Eastern Front, long before the rigours of the 'Hunger Winter' of 1944-45 and the going got really tough for everyone on the islands. To be fair to Lanz, however, he was not the only one to make such assumptions. Adolf Hitler, in the same midday 'table talk' in which he had advocated the islands becoming a marvellous health resort for the 'Strength through Joy' organisation, also commented that the inhabitants of the Islands considered themselves to be:

'... members of the British Empire rather than as subjects of the King, whom they still regard, not as King, but as the Duke of Normandy. If our occupation troops play their cards properly, we shall have no difficulties there.'[7]

Notes

1. OKW = *Oberkommando den Wehrmacht*, Germany's supreme command during the Second World War, based in Berlin and run by *Feldmarschall* Wilhelm Keitel.
2. Imperial War Museum Sound Archives, Accession No: 0010103/2
3. Imperial War Museum Sound Archives, Acession No: 10715/3/1
4. He would become the *Wehrmacht's* youngest *feldmarschall* in February 1943, but in Nov 1944 developed a brain tumor and was retired from active duty and died on 12 July 1945 whilst in American custody.
5. *'Dame of Sark an autobiography'* by Sibyl Hathaway
6. George Pope to this day remains a mysterious character, who appeared 'out of the blue' a day or two after the Germans arrived and 'disappeared' again after the Liberation, having worked throughout the period of the occupation for the Germans. Was he a spy – and if so for whom – the British or the Germans?
7. *Hitler's Table Talk.*

CHAPTER THREE

SETTLING IN – THE FIRST SIX MONTHS

A special time

The remaining months of 1940 were perhaps a special time in the history of the occupation of the Channel Islands. Whilst it was quite impossible for the soldiers who initially occupied the islands to have been in any way hand picked, they were certainly always on their best behaviour, generally friendly and genuinely tried to get on with the islanders. As one local historian commented:

> *'One of the most persistent of the many myths and legends that the Occupation generated was that the first German troops to land in the Channel Islands were obviously hand picked because they were all so good-looking, disciplined and polite. Nothing could have been further from the truth!' As we have already explained, 216 Infantry Division was chosen because it was the nearest division to Cherbourg and for no other reason. It was a division that had been formed out of the reservists of the Territorial Military Command from the Hanover area on 26 August 1939. Thus it was composed of well disciplined, healthy*

Normal battalion parades, like this one on Guernsey, were held as soon as the rest of 216.ID had arrived and the troops got down to garrison duties. Hans-Gerhard Sandmann

Spud bashing. Inevitably there were spuds to peel, both Jersey and Guernsey being famous for their potatoes.
Hans-Gerhard Sandmann

But there was also time to relax on the beautiful islands.
Hans-Gerhard Sandmann

young men, who had been taught to obey orders and who did so pleasantly and generally with a smile. So the: 'pre-Occupation purveyors of rape, pillage and wholesale looting rumours were sadly disappointed when it was found that the newly arrived troops went around saluting everything that moved, paying for all the items that they obtained in the shops and patting small children on the head.'[1]

Even the astute and worldly-wise Dame Sibyl Hathaway, who had so quickly seen through Maj Dr Maas' urbane charm, wrote in her autobiography:

'We found out later that the first troops sent to occupy the island were specially picked to impress on the British people that the Germans were well-behaved, well-disciplined and withal kind-hearted. The behaviour and discipline of these troops was excellent and it was rare to see a drunken German soldier in those early days.'

Rifle inspection. All infantrymen had to keep their rifles spotless, so they were regularly inspected. Sand and salt air did not make this easy as they affected the working parts of all weapons.

Guernsey Museum

From the soldiers point of view it was as though they had won first prize in the 'postings lottery'. While their compatriots were off to fight the Bolsevik hordes on the unknown steppes of Russia, they were here, garrisoning the beautiful Channel Islands, surrounded by shops that were still crammed with food and every conceivable luxury, much of which was already unobtainable back home. Besides, they were 'monarchs of all they surveyed', having beaten the best that the rest of Europe could assemble against them. Their morale was at an all-time high, so they had every reason to feel munificent towards the conquered peoples over whom they now ruled. Soon, they hoped, they would move on to capture England, so the need to build massive defensive fortifications had not yet arrived. They had only to bide their time and enjoy themselves.

This instruction is clearly about laying the Teller (lit: plate) mine, which weighed 91lbs, contained 11lbs of TNT and was 12 inches in diameter. It was primarily pressure detonated, but could be connected to other mines or set off by means of a tripwire.
Guernsey Museum

Get your haircut you idle soldier!
Guernsey Museum

Maj Lanz had a wide 'parish' to control. Here he is photographed with officers of both the army and navy during a visit to Sark.
(Guernsey Museum)

Occupying Forces

By the third week in July 1940, the military forces occupying the islands were as follows:

ARMY (*HEER*)

Guernsey

Island Commandant (*Inselkommandant*): Major Dr Albrecht Lanz. One infantry battalion (I./IR 396. ID 216), less detachments detailed below, plus one quarter of an anti-tank company (AT Kompanie) IR 396

Jersey

Island Commandant: *Hauptmann* Erich Gussek
One rifle company (*Schuetzen Kompanie*) of I./IR 396, half of a machine gun company (*Maschinengewehr Kompanie*) IR 396, quarter of an anti-tank company IR 396, one engineer platoon (*pionier zug*) 4.Pi/216 ID, one platoon cycle-borne (*radfahrer*) infantry

This 3.7cm Pak 35/36 L/45 is being set up in a coastal fire position somewhere on the islands. It was the most widely used German anti-tank gun and one of the best in its day, its effectiveness being improved by tungsten-cored AP40 ammunition after 1940.
BA via Société Jersiaise

A sentry on duty outside Maj Lanz's office in Guernsey, July 1940.
Guernsey Museum

A German sentry guards the entrance to Fort George, which the Germans took over as a barracks. Later in the war (in 1944) it was bombed and badly damaged.
Hans-Gerhard Sandmann

Alderney
Island Commandant: *Unterfeldwebel* Schmidt
One infantry platoon (*Schuetzen Zug*) of I./IR 396

Sark
Island Commandant: *Obergefrieter* Obenhauf
One infantry section (*Schuetzen Gruppe*) of I./IR 396

AIR FORCE (*LUFTWAFFE*)

During the early months the Luftwaffe personnel undoubtedly outnumbered those of the other two services. This was because of the need to use the airfields for staging and

An Me Bf 109 being refilled at the Guernsey airstrip in July 1940, using J H Miller's commandeered Commer truck as a petrol bowser! The pilot was 51 year old Hauptmann Wilhelm Meyerweissflog, who later during the Battle of Britain force-landed near Ramsgate. Michael Payne

A 'Flying Pencil', as the Dornier Do 17 was often called because of its thin pencil-like shape, is seen here just about to reach the rugged coastline of Guernsey. It was a four-seat medium bomber with a top speed of about 255mph. Guernsey Museum

Luftwaffe crews at La Villaze, Guernsey, make the most of the sun whilst waiting to scramble. The aircraft had to be well dispersed and camouflaged as RAF fighter-bombers often attacked them. Michael Payne

Initially only light weapons were available for defence – such as these twin MG 34s in an AA mounting (Zwillingssocket 36) The MG 34 was the most important German machine gun of the early war period, with a high rate of fire (8-900rpm) using a 50 round belt linked to form 250 rounds. BA via Société Jersiaise

refuelling of German aircraft taking part in the Battle of Britain. For example there were:

a. 24 x Light AA (*Flak*) guns – six 2cm Flak and six 3.7cm Flak on each of Jersey and Guernsey, mainly to protect the airfields, but also available for use against seaborne targets.

b. Fighter Groups JG 27 (*Jagdgruppe* 27) and JG 53 (Jagdgruppe 53), both operating at La Villiaze airport on Guernsey, JG 53 being the first to arrive. Both were equipped with Messerschmitt Bf109 single-seater fighters and are shown in the *Luftwaffe* Order of battle for *Adler Tag* (Eagle Day), the start of the Battle of Britain. Air activity declined after the *Luftwaffe* had lost the battle

c. Reconnaissance Group 123 (*Aufklarungsgruppe* 123) on Jersey. This long-range recce group was joined by the Messerschmitt Bf 110Cs of ZG 76 for the Battle of Britain, the

The Kriegsmarine was also represented in the Garrison, but initially the main naval coastal artillery and larger vessels were still to come. Instead, they were mainly small coastal trawlers as seen here at St Peter Port. However, as their range of armament shows, they could still give a good account of themselves.
IWM - HU 29101

This odd looking craft is a Flak ship, with its AA gun mounted on a perilous-looking platform high above the deck. Preumably it was for harbour protection, but one still wonders what it was like to be on board in bad weather! Guernsey Museum

small airfield rapidly becoming congested and having finally to be extended. When the Battle of Britain ended, the Henschel Hs126 and a few Dornier Do 17s were the main air activity, until the Henschels were replaced by the Fieseler Storch in 1941, which could practically fly backwards! Communication runs between islands and the mainland were the main activity.

d. **Airfield construction companies** (*Luftwaffe Baukompanie*) on both Gurnesey and Jersey to carry out enlargement work on the airfields.

NAVY (*KRIEGSMARINE*)

a. The naval assault group Gotenhafen was withdrawn once Op Green Arrow had been successfully concluded and moved to Paris for 'special employment'.

b. German naval harbour supervisory staff took over the port installations on the two main islands - and later on Alderney, requisitioning several small boats and taking over the cable stations. In due course this establishment would be increased and a Naval CinC Channel Islands (SEEKO-KI) established which was on a par with the other SEEKOs at Le Havre, Cherbourg, etc. His importance would be considerably greater when the naval artillery element of the garrison was vastly increased and it became one of the *Kriegsmarine* primary tasks

Later convoy escorts were provided by the 'ugly ducklings' of the German Navy – the artillery carriers (artillerietraeger), four of which operated in the Bay of St Malo and the Channel Islands area. They had a crew of fifty officers and men and carried the following weapons: 2 x 8.8cm guns, 2 x 2.7cm guns, 8 x 2.0cm AA guns and 1 x 1.5cm AA gun – a formidable array. Guernsey Museum

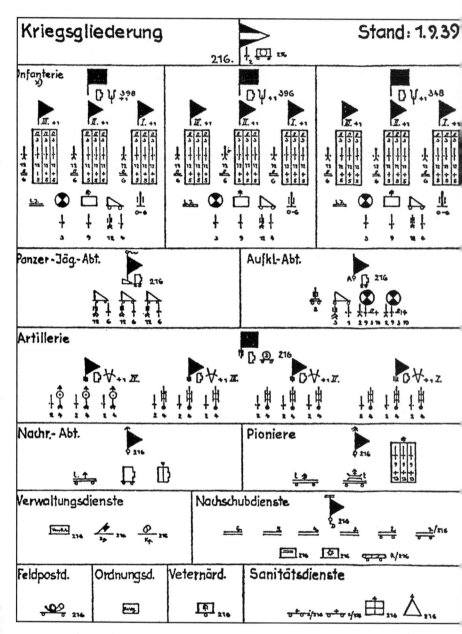

Kriegsgliederung

216.

Stand: 1.9.39

Infanterie

398 · 396 · 348

III. · II. · I.

Panzer-Jäg.-Abt. 216

Aufkl.-Abt. 216

Artillerie 216

Nachr.-Abt. 216

Pioniere 216

Verwaltungsdienste 216

Nachschubdienste 216

Feldpostd.

Ordnungsd.

Veternärd.

Sanitätsdienste 216

Organisational Chart for 216.Inf Div.

to prevent an enemy landing anywhere on the Channel Islands

c. The undersea cable which had been laid by the GPO in May 1940, was connected from Fliquet on Jersey, to Pirou on the Normandy coast. The Germans made several attempts during the occupation to lay a cable from Alderney to Cherbourg, but the rip of the tide always tore it out.

All in all, however, there were initially a very small number of German Servicemen to guard the newly-captured territory, which could and did lead to problems when British commandos carried out raids.

The arrival of *Feldkommand* 515

Almost as unwelcome to the military garrison as the incursions by British commandos, was the arrival in August 1940 of the German civil service bureaucrats who made up FK 515. This came about because the position of the Channel Islands within the overall scheme of all the occupied countries in Europe, was regularised that month and they were incorporated into the French Department of Manche (Channel) as a sub-district of Military Government Area A. Led by *Oberst* Friedrich Schumacher, the *Feldkommandant*, who arrived on the 9th August, FK 515 was divided into a series of departments dealing with such matters as the running of power, transportation, agriculture, etc. Its headquarters was established in Victoria College House, St Helier, Jersey, with offices in Guernsey and Alderney, plus an 'outpost' in Sark.

FK 515 staff were civilan personnel, but they wore uniform, were issued with pistols and ammunition and were required to carry out a certain amount of military training. There was considerable bad feeling between these bureaucrats 'the civilians in uniform' of the FK 515 and the 'fighting soldiers' of the garrison. This was not unique to the Channel Islands, however, because as the months progressed the need for a larger and larger garrison increased, so the pressure between the two groups became more and more difficult to control. As one historian put it:

> 'The Wehrmacht for their part made no secret of the fact that they despised the military government officials. Since they had little to do other than fire the anti-aircraft and coastal guns from time to time, there was plenty of opportunity for mutual resentment to build up.'[2]

A new military commander arrives

A sign that the Channel Islands were assuming more importance came the following month, when on 19 September, *Oberst Graf* (Colonel Baron) Rudolf von Schmettow arrived to set up his headquarters as *Befehlshaber der britische Kanalinseln (BdbK)* – Commander of the Channel Islands, above the two island commanders. Initially, his headquarters was on Jersey, first at 'Monaco' on St Saviour's Road, St Helier, then at the Metropole Hotel in Roseville Street. Von Schmettow was a man of great charm and humanity who had been born in Berlin on 8 January 1891. Joining the Army in 1909, he was commissioned into the cavalry in 1911, then after the First World War served in the *Reichsheer*, was an *Oberstleutnant* in 1935 and was promoted *Oberst* in 1938 (he would be promoted to General rank during his time in the Islands). He began the Second World War commanding Infantrie Regiment 164 in the 62. Infantrie Division, which did well in both Poland and France. He held the award of the German Cross in Gold and was by all accounts a pleasant man. One of his contemporaries on the Islands, Baron von Aufsess, the Head of Civil Affairs, described him as 'the little Saxon, who stuttered when he got excited!' He was a nephew of *Generalfeldmarschall* Gerd von Rundstedt and certainly built up a reputation for favouring the Islanders. He would remain as BdbK until the arrival of 319 ID in mid-July 1941, when the divisional commander *Generalmajor* Erich Mueller, who was thus senior to von Schmettow, became BdbK with his HQ in Guernsey. However, von Schmettow again became both BdbK and commander 319 ID, when Mueller was posted to the Eastern Front in 1943 and von Schmettow was promoted to replace him. His HQ was now very firmly in Guernsey, located in a large Georgian house called 'The Oberlands' at La Corbiere. The Organisation Todt would construct two command bunkers in the grounds and a barrack block to house the soldiers. He continued his liberal ways, one of the Garrision telling me:

> *'The General of the occupation division walked about without an escort and always had chocolate and sweets in his pockets for the children.'*

Unfortunately, as we shall see, his almost lenient approach made him the target for the more rabid Nazis on his staff, who

Another day at the office. A Guernsey policeman opens the car door for Major Albrecht Lanz, first German Commandant of the Channel Islands as he goes to his office as Der Deutsche Kommandant der Britischen Kanalinseln. (IWM - HU 616)

plotted to oust him and finally succeeded.

And Reinforcements

At the same time as the BdbK was established two new units arrived to strengthen the garrison, although initially as soon as they had taken over, the original infantry companies of IR 396 were recalled to the mainland. The two new units were: *Maschinengewehr* Bataillon (Machine Gun Battalion) 16 and *Panzerjaegerabteilung* (Anti-tank Battalion) 652. These two units were not integral parts of 216 ID, but rather GHQ troops which could be attached to any division for special duties. MG Btl 16 had been manning the machine gun posts in the Eifel district of the German/Belgian border. They had taken part in the battle for France as part of 1. *Kavallerie* Division, and their average age was 32, which was certainly higher than that of the troops they replaced. The anti-tank battalion's guns (3.7cm Pak 35/36) were now the largest anti-tank weapons on the Islands.

In addition men of the *Landschutz Bataillonen* IR 398 were drafted in to Jersey and Guernsey. Such battalions were classified as Home Defence Battalions and thus contained men who were older and less fit than the normal infantry. This was because, as well as manning the shoreline positions, there was now a mass of more mundane sentry duties to be performed, such as guarding fuel points, supply dumps, headquarters – even the residence of the BdbK, which could be tackled by an older age group. Also there was a major problem developing with the constant changeover of personnel between Islands which caused endless turbulence and difficulties, this could only be rectified by more reinforcement.

By the end of the year 1940 early 1941, the following reinforcements had arrived:

Guernsey – I., II., III./IR 398 to supplement MG Btl 16

Jersey – HQ Coy of I./IR 398, all of IV./IR 398, half of the AT Coy of IR 398, plus HQ and two Coys of *Pionier* Btl 216

Alderney – None, the island was still defended by the one platoon, but now from IR 348 (based at Cherbourg).

1941 would see major changes being mooted as Adolf Hitler began to take more interest in the defence of his 'Greater Germany'.

Notes

1. Michael Ginns, quoted from an article by him in the Channel Islands *Occupation Review* No 18 of 1990.
2. *The German Occupation of the Channel Islands* by Chartes Cruickshank

CHAPTER FOUR

1941 – THE YEAR OF CHANGE

A change of heart

After the stupendous victories of the early summer Germany undoubtedly put out peace feelers to the British, but these were totally rejected by Churchill's Government, who were now unwavering in their determination to pursue the war, despite the collapse of their major ally France. Clearly they would continue to fight, even if Great Britain was invaded and they had to carry on the struggle from overseas, somewhere in the Empire. The rescue of the British Expeditionary Force at Dunkirk changed the situation slightly, although Germany still had a considerable superiority of trained and equipped infantry and tank divisions, but lacked suitable shipping, in particular landing craft, to mount a successful invasion. Obviously there were, in any case, great risks in taking on such an operation and it would clearly have had more chance of success if overall strategic air superiority had been achieved in the Battle of Britain. However, the autumn of 1940 ended with the battered but undaunted Royal Air Force securing a major victory over the Luftwaffe and this was clearly an important factor in making Hitler change his mind and put the proposed invasion of Great Britain, Operation *Seeloewe* (Sealion) on hold. It was still a possibility and the threat had to be maintained, but as the months passed, the motivation for such an assault waned and a 'siege' of the British Isles with a concentrated attack on all supply routes, became the more favoured strategic option. It also allowed Hitler to turn his attentions eastwards onto his Soviet 'partners' whom he had all along seen as the real enemies of Fascism. Operation 'Barbarossa', the invasion of the Soviet Union, scheduled for June 1941, would now take priority and this would lead to some major changes in the West as well as in the East.

Although there was clearly no threat of a counter invasion by the British, and whilst the conquered countries of Euope did not themselves present an immediate problem, some suitable defensive structure would be necessary to hold everything

Reinforcements arrive by sea. After the initial assault operation most German servicemen arrived from France by sea. Here a boatload of coastal artillerymen arrive at St Peter Port, Guernsey.
Guernsey Museum

together, so that the might of the *Wehrmacht* could be employed in the East. The task of occupation was a very necessary one, but it could be done by second grade, older troops, rather than the young, virile soldiers who had captured Poland and France. This requirement led to the deliberate formation of a number of divisions – nine initially – destined from the outset as occupation forces.

A change of divisions

Thus one of the major happenings of 1941 on the Islands, was the change of the infantry division which was responsible for providing the main garrison troops, when ID 319 took over from ID 216. The troops of the new division had begun to arrive towards the end of March, although the official handover /takeover was scheduled as at 0001hrs 30 April, and some sub-units of 216 ID would remain until the summer of 1941. The well-behaved, good looking, young and well-disciplined soldiers of the 216th would soon find themselves on their way to the Eastern Front, where they were almost immediately involved in heavy fighting. In late 1941, they were disembarking from troop trains at Sukhinitchi – one of the Fourth Army's main ammunition dumps, when their division

The Germans relied on a proportion of bicycle troops, like these men in Guernsey. The bicycles were requisitioned from the civilian population, much to their annoyance. Guernsey Museum

was surrounded by the Soviet 10th Army. Only part of the division had actually arrived – some 4,000 troops in total – and with the assistance of another thousand supply troops and some Russian volunteers, they held the town against repeated enemy attacks. No doubt they would look back longingly to days spent

Everywhere there seemed to be soldiers marching about in their coal-scuttle helmets and jackboots, both 'Showing the Flag' or merely moving around the islands. These men were different being members of the RAD (Reicharbeitdienst) labour corps, in which everyone had to serve for six months before their military service. They would be used in the massive building projects. CIOS Jersey

on the golden beaches and leafy lanes of the Islands as they fought in snow and ice of the bitter Russian winter.

The incoming 319 ID had been formed at Gera on 15 November 1940, some sixteen months after 216 ID, in the 13th Wave of conscription, which, as already mentioned, had been aimed at creating nine new divisions for employment in occupied Europe. Thus from the outset it was seen as a static division, designed to man, for example, the fixed fortifications and weapons positions on what would soon become the Atlantic Wall. To start with it would also be responsible for St Malo and a sector of the French coast as well as the Islands, however, once Hitler had decided that the Allies would have to take the Islands before they could land on the French coast, 319 ID would be massively reinforced until it had become easily the largest infantry division in the German Army. This reinforcement will be covered later in its proper place, however, it is perhaps worth noting here that despite these increases, only a very small number of the original 319 ID personnel were actually left on the Islands for the entire period of the war, such were the continual demands of the voracious Eastern Front that even the static divisions were not left in peace. A conservative estimate made just before D Day, reckoned that only some 30% of the original divisional personnel was still serving on the

Listen to the Band! The various unit military bands often gave concerts which were listened to by the locals as well as the garrison. Guernsey Museum

Larger weaponry was now coming onto the island like this Flak 8.8cm, which is being manhandled into position. The '88' gained a fearsome reputation elsewhere in the anti-tank role, but this was of course secondary to its original AA role, when it had a crew of 10 men. IWM - HU 29053

Islands. General Walter Warlimont, Deputy Chief of *Oberkommando der Wehrmacht* (OKW) Operations Staff, in his book, *Inside Hitler's Headquarters 1939-45* confirms this continual drain, saying: 'Withdrawls to the East have been on a vast scale. 319 ID in the Channel Islands has only 30% of its original establishment', whilst *Generaloberst* Alfred Jodl commented: 'The best people have been removed.' Of course the vast size of 319 ID was an anathema to most soldiers – the rest of the army called them the 'Canada Division' as they reckoned it was certain that they would all finish up in Canadian POW camps Perhaps the most damning remarks were made by Warlimont who said that Hitler had: 'wrongly, uselessly and entirely for prestige purposes, left a complete infantry division on the Channel Islands.'

During its time in the Channel Islands, the division was initially commanded by *Generalleutnant* Erich Mueller who had been commanding since November 1940. Holder of the German Cross in Silver, he went on to become the Commandant of Danzig, then later commanded 603 ID until he was captured in August 1944. He ended the war in a Russian POW camp where he remained until 1955. His successor was, as already mentioned, the amiable *Generalleutnant* Graf Rudolf von

Schmettow, who, as BdbK was promoted into the post, but was summarily 'retired' when the rabid Nazi *Vizeadmiral* Huffmeier took over as BdbK. However, von Schmettow not only survived the war but also visited the Channel Islands as a tourist postwar. He would hand over command of the division temporarily to *Oberst* Heine who was later replaced by *Generalmajor* Rudolf Wulf, holder of the Knight's Cross with Oakleaves, who took over the division on 1 March 1945 and surrendered with his division at the end of the Occupation.

The basic organization of 319 ID, before reinforcement, was very similar to that of 216 ID, namely, three infantry regiments (IR 582, IR 583 and IR 584), one artillery regiment (AR 319), an anti-tank battalion, an engineer battalion, a reconnaissance company and a signal company, all of which took the 319 prefix. Although there was a certain amount of 'to-ing and fro-ing' – for example, initially divisional HQ, the engineer battalion and IR 583 stayed in Normandy, the infantry holding a defensive position centered around the River Vire area, the three infantry regiments eventually all ended up on the Islands with IR 582 stationed in Jersey, whilst IR 583 and IR 584 were in Guernsey. The other major unit which had been part of the original garrison was Machine Gun Battalion 16 and once the three new infantry regiments were properly established, MGBtl 16 moved to Jersey and stayed there for the rest of the war.

The 'Gibraltar of the Channel'

Although as yet not significant enough to earn itself the title of 'Gibraltar of the Channel' which the Germans would bestow, the small island of Alderney was starting to assume considerable importance. This was partly due to the fact that it was nearer to France than it was to the other Channel Islands, being only 15 miles from Cherbourg, yet 25 miles from Guernsey and 40 miles from Jersey. It therefore seemed more logical to the Germans that Alderney should be garrisoned by the division occupying the Cherbourg area, which was now 83 Infantry Division, since 216 ID had been posted to the Eastern Front. Therefore, they took over Alderney and by June 1941, had a garrison there of some 450 men. At the end of July, the reinforced 5 Company of 277 Infantry Regiment (83 ID regiments were 251, 257 and 277) arrived, under a *Hauptmann* Carl Hofmann, who became the Island Commandant with his

The building of coastal defensive positions, such as these bunkers at Noirmont Point, Jersey, was begun in April 1941, when Hitler turned his attention on fortifying the islands. This work is being done by troops of a construction battalion, plus local workers. Société Jersiaise

headquarters at the Connaught Hotel, St Anne. From then on the garrison ballooned, there being over 2,000 German servicemen on Alderney by November 1941 (1,100 army, 1,100 air force and some 200 sailors). Soon these figures would pass the 3,000 mark, not counting the first Organization Todt labour contingent that was about to arrive. Hofmann would lose his post to an *Oberst* Gleden, then, a few weeks later, at the beginning of the New Year, command would be passed over to 319 Infantry Division.

Hitler orders the fortification of the Channel Islands

The Fuehrer had always taken a great personal interest in the Channel Islands ever since their capture, but in mid-1941 and despite being heavily involved in the final stages of planning 'Barbarossa', he made up his mind that the islands would have to be both heavily fortified and heavily garrisoned. Quoting from General Walter Warlimont again, he says that there were worries that Britain and the rest of the Allies might mount some sort of retaliatory action to help Russia:

'The time had now arrived ... when plans and prospects of German strategy had to be re-examined. Directive No 33 dated 19 July, had contained an instruction of the type to which in those days we had become unaccustomed: in the West and North,

the possibility of attacks on the Channel Islands and the Norwegian coast must be borne in mind.'

Hitler's fortification order of 20 October 1941

Hitler's wishes were put into effect when the following directive (see below) was issued by the Fuehrer's office. It offically 'rubber stamped' the decisions which had been made at a series of high level conferences that had been taking place in Berlin since early in 1941. Whilst these conferences were in progress, the military engineers had been looking very carefully at the Islands. The order read:

1. Operations on a large scale against the territories we occupy in the West are, as before, unlikely. Under pressure of the situation in the East, however, or for reasons of politics or propaganda, small scale operations at any moment may be anticipated, particularly an attempt to regain possession of the Channel Islands, which are important to us for the protection of sea communications.

2. Counter-measures in the Islands must ensure that any English attack fails before a landing is achieved, whether it is attempted by sea, by air or both together. The possibility of advantage being taken by bad visibility to effect a surprise landing must be borne in mind. Emergency measures for strengthening the defences have already been ordered, and all branches of the forces stationed in the Islands, except for the Air Force, are placed under the orders of the Commandant of the Islands.

3. With regard to the permanent fortifications of the Islands, to convert them into an impregnable fortress (which must be pressed forward with the utmost speed) I give the following orders:

a. The High Command of the Army is responsible for the fortifications as a whole and will, in the overall programme, incorporate the construction for the Air Force and the Navy. The strength of the fortifications and the order in which they are erected will be based on the principles and the practical knowledge gained from building the Western Wall (ie: the Siegfried Line).

b. For the Army: it is important to provide a close network of emplacements, well concealed, and given flanking fields of fire. The emplacements must be sufficient for guns of a size capable of piercing armour plate 100cm thick, to defend against tanks which may attempt to land. There must be ample accomodation for stores and ammunition, for mobile diversion parties and for armoured cars.

c. For the Navy: one heavy battery on the Islands and two on the French coast to safeguard the sea approaches. (This was to be the heavy battery on Guernsey – Batterie Mirus. The two on the mainland were to be on the Joburg Peninsula and near Paimpol on the Brittany coast, but they were never installed, two 20.3cm railway guns being put there instead -one in each location).

d. For the Air Force: strongpoints must be created with searchlights and sufficient to accommodate such AA units as are needed to protect all important constructions.

e. Foreign labour, especially Russians and Spaniards but also Frenchmen, may be used for the building works.

4. Another order will follow for the deportation to the Continent of all Englishmen who are not natives of the Islands, ie not born there.

5. Progress reports to be sent to me on the first day of each month, to the C-in-C of the Army and directed to the Supreme Command of the Armd Forces (OKW) – Staff of the Fuehrer, Division L.

(signed) ADOLF HITLER

(Source: Channel Islands Occupation Review 1973 and published here by kind permission of CIOS (Jersey)

The military engineers arrive

At the head of the military engineers who had been visiting the Islands for many months was *Generalleutenant* Rudolf Schmetzer, who spent his entire wartime career in the fortification business. He was Inspector *Landbefestig West* from 15 Aug 40 until 1 Apr 44 and was allocated two Fortress Engineer Staffs (*Festungs Pionier Stab*) – XIV for Jersey

Members of the Organisation Todt wore mainly Czech khaki uniforms, with distinctive ORGANIZATION TODT armbands. The man in the front was the boss of the OT workers who built many of the bunkers on Guernsey.
Werner Wagenknecht

Officers of Festpistab 14 (Jersey) – Fortress Engineers – posing outside their HQ at the Grand Hotel Jersey. In the centre of the three seated is OTL Eimler, the commanding officer, whilst standing on the extreme left is Olt Professor Walther Kluepfel, an eminent geologist, who was responsible for the siting of all tunnels and OT camps. Société Jersiaise

and XIX for Guernsey – which comprised teams of experts who made geological, geographical and strategic surveys of the Islands, then put forward their recommendations regarding the siting of observation towers, gun positions, strongpoints, control towers, etc. In their reports they commented upon the excellence of the granite fortifications which had been built in the Napoleonic days – and earlier, saying that they were extremely well built, sited in the best possible strategic positions and need only some additional reinforced concrete to make them suitable for modern warfare. Schmetzer left the Islands at the end of 1941, to supervise the construction of the entire Atlantic Wall[1] and his place was taken by *Oberstleutnant* von Marnitz from the Jersey Fortress Engineer Staff.

And the Organization Todt

Another famous (or should it be infamous?) visitor was Dr Fritz Todt, head of Organization Todt, who came in November 1941, when the first of his workers arrived. Born in Pforzheim,

Baden, in September 1891, the son of a jewellery factory owner, he had won the Iron Cross during World War One and was wounded whilst flying as an observer. Postwar he joined the Munich firm of Sager and Woerner, which specialized in building roads and tunnels, rising to become their manager. Soon after Hitler came to power Todt was made head of the new state-owned *Reichsautobahnen* corporation and directed the building of the new road system which had been laid out by the military planners. He helped to found the *Nationalsozialisticher Bund deutscher Technik* and during World War Two, this quiet, withdrawn technocrat, held three major positions: Minister of Armaments & Munitions; Head of the Organization Todt; and from late 1941, responsibility for restoring the road and rail system in occupied Russia. He was killed in an aeroplane accident on the Eastern Front in February 1942, when his He 111 exploded killing all on board. Sabotage was naturally suspected although no evidence was ever found. However, it is interesting to note that his successor, the Fuehrer's favourite architect, Albert Speer, who was due to be on the same flight, had cancelled at the last minute.

Who did what. Before explaining briefly the way in which the OT operated, we must delineate their responsibilities in the overall construction of fortifications on the Islands. They did not

Men of an Austrian construction battalion drag a heavy naval coastal gun up into its position at Fort Albert, Alderney, June 1941.
Alderney Society and Museum

just take over everything but were only one of the five main elements concerned with the building programme. These were:

a. Individual Units & Subunits. The soldiers on the ground were responsible for the construction of their own individual weapon pits, foxholes and trenches.

b. Divisional Engineer Units. They were concerned with the distribution, recording and sowing of landmines, also, the location and use of flamethrowers.

c. Army Construction Battalions. They were responsible for the construction of reinforced field works that were designed to give protection against small-arms fire, shell splinters and the like, but not against prolonged bombardment. Where concrete was used it did not exceed one metre in thickness.

d. Fortress Engineers and Fortress Construction Battalions. The supplying and mounting of fortress weapons, moving very heavy loads, some tunneling, compiling construction progress reports and maps, ordering and supervising tasks undertaken by the OT.

e. Organization Todt. Quarrying, most tunneling projects, constructing power stations, railways and roads, supplying building equipment and machinery, organising sea transport (in conjunction with the Kriegsmarine), loading and unloading ships, supervising civilian construction firms, controlling non-military labour and building fortress-type constructions (built of reinforced concrete not less than two metres thick).

(Source: CIOS Jersey Archive Book No 8)

Org. Todt

ORGANIZATION TODT (OT)

Although they were civilians, the German OT personnel wore uniform. This was mainly captured Czech khaki rather than normal Heer uniforms, as the photographs clearly show, although Dr Fritz Todt mainly wore Luftwaffe uniform as he held the honorary rank of *General der Flieger*. They filled the posts of foremen, camp administrators and officials. They were subject to military law, had 'paramilitary' status, so were allowed access to military facilities. They had a similar chain of command to the military – see table below – and their ranks can be equated as the second table shows (page 72).

CHAIN OF COMMAND OT

Einsatzgruppen West
(Western Europe)
|

Oberbauleitung (OBL) Normandie
(Based at St Malo. In February 1943, Alderney came under OBL Cherbourg)
|

Abschnitt Jersey	Abschnitt Guernsey	Abschnitt Alderney
3 x Baustelle	2 x Baustelle	3 x Baustelle

RANKS OF OT AND THEIR APPROXIMATE MILITARY EQUIVALENT
Badges of Rank

The OT expanded rapidly, recruiting large numbers of foreigners, but relatively few Germans (whose average age was 53). Some 80% of OT members were thus young non-Germans, enticed in by clever propaganda. Nevertheless, large numbers of German civilian building contractors were also arriving in the Channel Islands to work for the OT, for example, one sharp-eyed observer, newspaperman Leslie Sinel, recorded in his secret diary, that in November 1941:

> *'Germans are absolutely pouring in, including civilians; stores are arriving galore and there were over forty different steamers and barges in the harbour today (7 November 1941), all unloading. German building firms are trying to get labour, and more builders are springing up with the Island becoming more and more a German armed camp.'*

71

Organization Todt Badges and Ranks

T-Arbeiter
T-Sanitäter
T-Stammarbeiter

OT-Vorarbeiter
OT-Stammsanitäter

OT-Meister
OT-Obersanitäter

O-Obermeister
OT-Hauptsanitäter

OT-Truppführer
OT-Sanitätstruppführer

OT-Obertruppführer
OT-Sanitätsobertruppführer

OT-Haupttruppführer
OT-Sanitätshauptführer

OT-Bauführer
OT-Frontführer
OT-Arzt

OT-Oberbauführer
OT-Oberfrontführer
OT-Oberarzt

OT-Hauptbauführer
OT-Hauptfrontführer
OT-Stabsarzt

OT-Bauleiter
OT-Stabsfrontführer
OT-Oberstabsarzt

OT-Oberbauleiter
OT-Oberstabsfrontführer
OT-Oberfeldarzt

OT-Hauptbauleiter
OT-Oberstfrontführer
OT-Oberstarzt

OT-Einsatzleiter

OT-Einsatzgruppenleiter II

OT-Einsatzgruppenleiter I

72

And the Workers

This quasi-military force did give employment to some workers from amongst the population of the Islands, as the example posters show. However, the vast majority of their workforce were the poor unfortunates who had been unwillingly swept into 'the system' as slave labour. Among these there were distinct levels of nastiness, but all the workers, irrespective of the country of origin were inevitably treated with the same casual brutality which infected almost everything touched by the Nazis. They contained, for example, as Hitler's Fortification Order allowed, viz: '... Foreign labour, especially Russians and Spaniards, but also Frenchmen, may be used for the building works.' This gave to OT *carte blanche* to use anyone they wished, and, as we shall see, led to such acts of brutality – especially on the 'closed' island of Alderney, that it is difficult to find words to express one's revulsion towards the perpetrators. Of course the worst of all were the SS who ran some of the labour camps on Alderney, but the OT as a whole must bear their share of the blame, hence my remarks about its head, Fritz Todt. The prestigious *Oxford Companion to the Second World War* comments of the OT:

> *'They were technicians, slave-drivers and in some cases murderers. Their technical ability was doubtless greater than their discipline... they were not just "soldier-workers" but part of the Nazi system of terror and annihilation. Its members were committed in anti-partisan campaigns and supervised teams of Jewish slave-workers and Soviet POW.'*

By 1944, corruption was rife within the OT, as were other unmistakable signs of oganizational deregeneration. After the German defeat the OT was broken up and banned.

Juan Taule was typical of the non-German forced labourers, who was 'acquired' by the OT. He had fought in the Spanish Civil War, escaped over the frontier into France and was 'given' (his own words) to the Germans by the French in late 1940. He was initially employed working on the submarine base at La Rochelle, but after some six months was taken over to Jersey and billeted in St Elizabeth Castle. He worked on the sea walls around the castle initally, then moved to various locations, staying longest at Camp Udet, Route de Orange, working on bunkers and the sea wall at La Carriere Point, St Ouen's Bay, etc. Working conditions were not good and food was scarce,

This is the gun pictured on page 69, being dragged into position. It was one of three 17cm SK L/40 naval guns which made up Batterie Elsass and had a range of 22kms. Alderney Society & Museum

especially in 1943. Fortunately, the foreman, who was with the gang all the way through was: '... one of the good Germans' and treated them reasonably well: 'we were lucky to get him', commented Mr Taule.

The OT conscripted and then brought in building contractors from Germany and elsewhere on the Continent to work for them and Juan Taule actually worked for Kehl & Co from Germany. 'Germans are absoluetly pouring in,' commented one civilian observer in November 1941,

> *'including civilians, stores are arriving galore and there are over forty different steamers and barges in the harbour today, all unloading. German building firms are trying to get more labour, and more builders are springing up with the Island becoming more and more a German armed camp.'[2]*

The States of Jersey Department of Labour had tried to prevent local men from having to seek work from the Germans, by starting a number of innovative schemes, such as forestry, road building and clearing streams so as to harness their water power to run old mills, but the problem was that the German authorities put a ceiling on the wages that could be paid for such work, which were far too low for anyone to be able to maintain a family. Then the OT offered to pay wages at least double the ceiling, just for driving lorries, so it was no real surprise that over 500 local men volunteered to work for them.

September, 1941 and
the newly arrived firm
of Theodor Elsche
advertises for workers.

Warning of
escaped
prisoner.

Search for
wanted
persons.

On the civilian front

'However bitter the aftermath of a successful invasion, sooner or later some form of civil government would have had to be set up in the conquered British Isles, and some method of working with the Germans would have had to be evolved, however, reluctant and however much those old enough to remember a time when there were no Germans in the streets, longed for liberation.'

That quotation comes from Norman Longmate's fascinating book: *If Britain had fallen* in which he deals with the hypothetical situation of a successful German conquest of Great Britain. Of course it was not hypothetical as far as the Channel Islanders were concerned, they had to continue to keep the Islands functioning no matter what happened. I am therefore continually annoyed by the way in which some historians are inclined to make snide remarks about how the 'Model Occupation', as some have called it, actually worked. Not so Norman Longmate. Towards the end of his book, when writing about the actual occupation of the Channel Islands rather than the hypothetical one of Great Britain which he had been describing, he says:

'During five years, when it must often have seemed that they had been forgotten and that the war would last for ever, the loyalty of the people of the Channel Islands to their own race and their own country, their pride in their past and their faith in the future never wavered.'

That is I believe, a fair description if the way in which the majority of the Islanders behaved. For example, when asked about the attitude of the average civilian once the Occupation got under way, whether they would snub the Germans or be friendly and co-operative towards them, Leslie Sinel, a Jersey newspaper reporter replied:

'No, I won't say co-operate – but you had to work with them according to where you were, they took over places and you had to work with them, but that's not to say you were friendly. At the office were some Germans running their newspaper and in normal times you could have – they were quite likeable some of them – but obviously you did not entertain them. There were a few isolated cases but basically nobody entertained the Germans or got overfriendly except where they thought they could get something out of them. An empty belly had no conscience and

*when food got short, if there was a chance of getting something
it was obvious you forgot your scruples and you had something
extra'.*[3]

It was clearly a very difficult job for those who had to be in daily
contact with the Germans to walk the narrow path between co-
operation and non-co-operation, when so many lives depended
upon maintaining the delicate balance. Mundane but important
matters such as bread rationing (March 1941), milk rationing
(August 1941) and fuel rationing (December 1941), which
affected every member of the population had to be dealt with,
as well as more unpalatable, delicate matters like the
deportation of Jews and then of Englishmen. I believe that the
vast majority of Channel Islands civil servants were decent,
honourable men, who on occasions were forced to make some
unpalatable decisions, affecting the few and behalf of the many.
Raymond Falla, for example, was a member of the purchasing
commission, which contained both Channel Islands and
German representation, who bought urgent supplies from
France – both offically and clandestinely via the Black Market.
Consequently he routinely risked prosecution by the Germans
for his black market activities, but somehow managed to
hoodwink them throughout his time with the commission. He
puts this down to the studious regard which the Germans had
for the sanctity of orders:

*'"Befehl ist Befehl, Herr Falla!" (Orders are Orders Mr
Falla) they would say, and once they knew what the order was,
the German mind did not deviate. He doesn't react to changes of
circumstance very quickly, so you were safe in spoofing them a
bit'*[4].

He also found himself in trouble and threatened with deportation for complaining that German soldiers were stealing farm
goods and animals, so he always had to gauge how far he could
go before he got into deep water.

From the German side it was, for the average soldier, just as
difficult. One told me:

*'We could not make any really good contacts with the
inhabitants of Guernsey, but I know it was wartime and we the
aggressors. So the only possible way was to co-exist was to be
absolutely correct, and if possible helpful to the other side and I
think that most people did so.'*

Another recalled how a farmer near his quarters with whom he

Sonderfuehrer Hohl, at work with Mr H Grube of the Jersey Evening Post. Hohl was the first censor and the civilian staff had constant battles with him. He and his successors insisted that their translations of German propaganda be published word for word, with the result that some contained really comical 'howlers'! All in all it was a difficult time for the staff of both the main islands newspapers. (There were various grades of Sonderfuehrer for which there is no direct British equivalent, as they were a device enabling rank to be held by those whose service was necessary but who were not actually serving members of the Wehrmacht).
Société Jersiaise

was quite friendly had commented:

> 'I love your singing when you march off in the morning to your exercises. It sounds great. But, by gum, I wish you would go all the same. Because it would be nice to be free again!'[5]

Notes

1. The Atlantic Wall: This was the series of coastal defensive fortifications which the Germans constructed, extending for over 2,600kms from North Cape in the Arctic Circle to the Spanish/French border. Later it was extended towards Petsamo in Finland.

2. Quoted in *The Organisation Todt and the Fortress Engineers in the Channel Islands* by Michael Ginns

3. IWM Sound Records Archive Accession No 010066/2.

4. IWM Sound Records Archive Accession No 01000/4

5. IWM Sound Records Archive Accession No 010006/8

CHAPTER FIVE

1942 – MORE MEN AND MORE BUILDING

Directive No 40 of 23 March 1942

In addition to Hitler's Fortification Order of 20 October 1941, another of the many orders issued by his headquarters, Directive No 40 of 23 March 1942, had a major effect upon the defence of the Islands, giving the primary responsibility of preventing an enemy landing to the *Kriegsmarine*. Only once the enemy had landed did it become the responsibility of the *Heer*. Naval artillery, which would thus provide the vital initial strike against any attempted landing, is covered in the next chapter. First of all, however, we must deal with army reinforcements

Army Reinforcements – Infantry

As we have already seen, the result of Hitler's order to turn the Channel Islands into 'The Mailed Fist of the Atlantic Wall' as German propaganda colourfully described the fortification of the Islands, was to order in the entire 319 Infantry Division

This 10.5cm K 331(f) gun crew is made up of Russians from 823 Georgian Battalion (Ostbataillon 823). They did not operate as a single unit, but rather were used to make up numbers. Attempts were made to recruit from amongst the Russian slave workers, but without success. IWM - HU 29157

towards the late autumn of 1941. The division was subsequently reinforced by a mixture of troops, which included two battalions of ex-Red Army soldiers, who had switched their allegiance, namely: *Ostbataillon* 823 which was composed of men from the Georgian Legion, who went to Guernsey; and *Ostbataillon* 643 containing men of the Russian Liberation Army who went to Jersey. They did not operate as complete units, but rather were used to make up numbers and to balance out the inevitable lack of experience amongst new recruits and the 'middle age ailments' of the older men in the infantry battalions. Fruitless efforts were made to recruit more Russians from among the slave workers.

Field Artillery

It was not only the incoming infantry regiments that were short of weapons and manpower. *Artillerieregiment* 319, had also to be brought up to strength and then given an extra battalion of twelve guns. However, all its weapons were of Czech origin, rather than German, so instead of the normal 10.5cm gun howitzers its batteries were equipped with either 8cm LK 30(t) which had been the Skoda 76.5mm M.30(NPK), or the 10cm

Field artillery weapons were mainly 10.5cm or 8cm and came from various occupied countries like Czechoslovakia and France rather than from Germany. This is a French 105mle 1913 Schneider, known in German parlance as the K331(f). It was used on all three of the main islands for harbour protection. (IWM - HU 29033)

leFH 14/19(t) which had been the Skoda 100mm Model 14/19. The extra battalion was most necessary as the artillery had to be spread over the three main islands.

The artillery did not all arrive at the same time and, as with the infantry, there was a certain amount of moving around to cover perceived threats until its full strength had been achieved, when the layout was as follows:

a. *Battle HQ* (*Kernwerk*) was at L'Aleval on Jersey, whilst CO AR 319 was ARKO (*Artillerie-Kommandeur*) Jersey. His four batteries were located:

b. **JERSEY**
I./AR 319 - HQ at St Brelade with batteries as follows:
Derflinger (unnumbered) – at Mont de la Rocque, St Brelade (2 x 8cm FK30(t))
Fritsch (No 1 Bty) – at Mont Cambrai (4 x 10cm le FH14/19(t))
Seydlitz (No 2 Bty) – at Mont du Coin (4 x 8cm FK 30(t))
Ziethen (No 3 Bty) – at L'Oeillòre, St Brelade (4 x 10cm le FH14/19(t))
II./AR 319 – HQ at Mont Mallet (Victoria Tower) Gorey with batteries as follows:
Seeckt (No 4 Bty) – at Rue de Blancq, St Clement (4 x 10cm le FH14/19(t))
Dietl (No 5 Bty) – at Maufant Rd, St Saviour (4 x 10cm le FH14/19(t))
Brauchitsch (No 6 Bty) – at Daisy Hill, Gorey (4 x 10cm le FH14/19(t))

c. **GUERNSEY AND ALDERNEY** (all on Guernsey except as shown)
III./AR 319 – HQ at Les Vardes, St Peter Port, with batteries as follows:
Georgfeste (No 7 Bty) – at Fort George (4 x 10cm le FH14/19(t))
Sperber (No 8 Bty) – at Delancey Park (4 x 10cm le FH14/19(t))
Tiger (No 9 Bty) – at Best's Brickyard (4 x 10cm le FH14/19(t))
IV./AR319 – HQ at Les Eturs House, with batteries as follows:

Wolf (No 10 Bty) – at Talbot Valley (4 x 10cm le FH14/19(t))
Falke (No 11 Bty) – at St Anne, Alderney (4 x 10cm le FH14/19(t))
Lux (No 12 Bty) – at Mont Saint (4 x 10cm le FH14/19(t))

(Source: *CIOS Review* (Jersey) May 1975, which makes the point that this layout was not fully finalised until September 1944)

Fire Direction control for these batteries was co-ordinated and run via the various naval direction and rangefinding positions *(Marinenpeilstande (MP)* which are explained later.

Anti-tank Artillery

Panzerjaegerabteilung (PzJgAbt) 319 was concentrated in Jersey, where it provided a mobile reserve, being reinforced with fifteen self-propelled artillery (Czech 4.7cm Pak guns mounted on the Renault tank chassis, known in German parlance as the 4.7cm Pak(t) auf PzKpfw 35R (f)). They had arrived during 1942. There was insufficient anti-tank artillery to spread to Guernsey, so a second battalion PzJgAbt 225 from 225 ID was sent in. The rest of the division, which had been on occupation duties in France, was sent off to the Eastern Front, so the anti-tank gunners had a lucky escape. Both battalions were obvious choices as mobile reserves on both islands and were renamed accordingly: PzJgAbt 225 became *Schnell Abteilung* 450 (Schnell

The other main AFV was the 4.7cm Pak 36(t) auf GW Renault 35(t), self-propelled anti-tank gun, which was used as mobile reserve on both islands. (IWM - HU 29031)

= fast) on 3 October 1942, while PzJgAbt 319 became *Schnell Abteilung* 319 on the same day.

In addition to the integral divisional artillery, various coastal artillery units (*Heeres Kuesten Artillerie*) would be sent over to man some of the mass of coastal guns pouring in to the Islands. However, as they did not start to arrive until May 1943, they will be covered in the next chapter.

Tanks

Probably the most incongruous weapons to be sent to the Islands were tanks, especially as they were captured French equipment, not German AFVs at all. And to make matters worse, the first consignment were First World War vintage Renault FT 17s. These had arrived in small numbers on all three islands in the middle of 1941, the FT 17 having been obsolete since the early 1930s, so they would have been precious little good against modern AFVs. However, in March 1942 *Panzerabteilung* 213 (Pzabt) arrived. They were equipped with

First of the tanks to arrive were these vintage Great War French FT 17s. Both Guernsey and Jersey received eight each, whilst Alderney got four. Badly armoured, mechanically unreliable and armed only with a machine gun, they were obsolete before the war started. When the Char B1 bis arrived they were relegated to secondary tasks, those in Jersey, for example, being used by the infantry for airfield defence. By the end of 1944 very few were still in running order. (Both Guernsey Museum)

Much better, more modern tanks eventually arrived. They were the thirty six Renault Char B1 bis which were divided between Guernsey and Jersey. Most were gun tanks but they included ten flamethrowing versions (five to each island). They all belonged to Panzerabteilung 213. (IWM - HU29034)

what had been one of the largest, heaviest and best armed tanks of the Blitzkrieg era, the French *Char* B1bis. Three hundred and sixty five had been built for the French Army and large numbers had been subsequently captured by the Germans. Pzabt 213 had been converted onto all French equipment – tanks, lorries, even motorcycles and warned for service with Rommel's *Deutsches Afrika Korps*, but in early 1942, this had been changed to the Channel Islands. The total strength of PzKpfw *Char* B1 bis (f) was 36 tanks and they were divided between the two main islands as follows:

Guernsey – Bn HQ – 2 x command version tanks
        No 2 Company – 12 x normal gun tanks and 5 x
        flamethrowing tanks
Jersey – No 1 Company – ditto

(The normal armament was a 75mm gun, low down in the hull and a 47mm in the turret, plus two machine guns. The flamethrower had a flame gun fitted instead of the 75mm hull gun and was known as the PzKpw B1 *bis mit Flammwerfer*.

They would thus be the only German panzer battalion never to see action.

A soldier's life

The duties of an average member of the garrison were fairly mundane and it must have been hard to keep up morale and

84

ensure that the soldiers were always 'in their toes'. This description is by the late Georg Brefka, who served as a member of MGBtl 16 in Jersey, rotating around various strongpoints, although he spent most of his time manning what was known as 'Resistance Nest Les Brayes'. He writes:

'The day was long, beginning at 6am and at 10pm we had our rest. At 7am, after breakfast, work began, there was construction of positions, cleaning of arms and ammunition, and training with guns and weapons. About every four weeks there was practice shooting with live ammunition at targets. These were sheets of lead which had been set up in the bay. Sometimes there was also night shooting with the aid of a searchlight. The rust produced by the strong salt content of the air caused great difficulties for the equipment. But the sand was much worse. Since the greater part of the installation lay in the dunes of the Bay, sand was to be found everywhere and always! While constructing positions or doing work, barbed wire was continuously being put around the installation. Trenches for communication and protection were dug, improved and camouflaged. Sods of grass were used for camouflage, they were cut out from somewhere on the other side of the road and transported in handcarts. The position was then more difficult to see and the sand from the dunes was also covered up. A problem of a particular kind was presented by sentry duty. Normally at night, or during the hours of darkness, three men did sentry duty. One was in front on the road while the other two patrolled as a double watch throughout the area, ie: the communication trenches at the bunker and as far as the wall at the beach. During the day there was only one sentry who stayed by the entrance on the road. I have no pleasant memories of sentry duty. Normally we had to do two turns of two hours and twenty minutes every night – only about every fifth night did we not have to do more than one turn of sentry duty. There were only a few of us, and when we thought that nothing was going to happen, for example, when it was stormy or there was a very high tide, we slept a little while on sentry duty, sometimes sleeping standing without falling down. And all of this despite the fear of a German court martial on the one hand and of British commandos on the other. We were on the move the whole day and then out twice a night as well, with never a free night. We were all very tired. And we were checked every night. The positions of the Second Company

Soldatenheim. Catering for the general welfare of the troops were these small rest and recreation centres, which mostly had a canteen and some shopping facilities. This one was in Alderney off Connaught Square in St Anne.
(Alderney Society and Museum)

were checked by the First Company and vice versa.

'At Les Brayes there was also a trained dog with a handler and they took part in checking too. When the tide was low La Rocco Tower also had to be checked, in case of landings by British commandos. On the tower, a French 30.5cm naval shell had been installed which could be set off from Les Brayes by remote control by means of an electric cable. The combat bunker near the slip was only there for emergency and was only used for sleeping. Some troops slept in a former anti-tank gun garage which was made of corrugated iron and dug into the sand. For daytime living and our sparse free time, there was a big wooden hut available and our meals were taken here too. The food was brought from the La Moye Golf Hotel every day by two or three men and carried on their backs in sacks or cans. There was no drinking water available in the Resistance Nest. Thousands of bottles of mineral water had to be stored in case of emergency. Normally fresh water was fetched from a deep bunker that had been cosntructed by OT workers, in this was a spring with a hand pump. It was situated half way to La Pulente on the left-hand side of the road, it must still be there today.

'Only particularly heavy things were brought from La Moye by horse and cart. A lorry was there for emergency use, but I did not see it being driven until after the capitulation. Every Saturday, everybody had to go from Les Brayes to La Moye for a shower – that was an order. The quietest day was Sunday – in the morning clothes were cleaned and tidied; after lunch we were free and some of the personnel were allowed to go to St Brelade's

Bay to the church service or the *Soldatenheim (Soldier's Home –
a type of club)*, where there was a very nice bookshop among
other things. In addition, field religious services were
occasionally held in the wooden hut.'

Comforts for the troops

In addition to the *Soldatenheime*, which were established on
all the Islands and were not unlike the British voluntary clubs
run by the Toc H and Church Army, although they could also be
likened to the NAAFI and the American PX, there were other
establishments such as *Soldatenkaufhaueser* (soldiers' shops)
opened in 1942 in both Jersey and Guernsey, where servicemen
could buy two very different types of goods. One were personal
necessities – razor blades, shaving brushes, toothbrushes and
toothpaste etc, whilst at the other end of the spectrum were
luxury goods – perfume, silk underwear, stockings etc, intended
for them to send home to wives and girlfriends, or to take home
when they went on leave. The shops did a good trade but there
were grumbles from those servicemen who lived too far away
from them. By the end of 1944, supplies had dried up and the
shops closed.

Also opening in St Peter Port and St Helier were *Freudenhaus*
(house of joy) where *die Prostituierte* were employed in the
German official brothels. Each had a staff of approximately two
men and thirteen women, all of whom were brought over from
France. Later, more brothels were opened, including an OT one
in Alderney. The women were provided with civilian ration
books on the orders of the FK 515 and classed as 'heavy
workers'. One civilian observer commented:

*'The queues of customers waiting in the gardens of the chosen
houses offered a certain amount of innocent amusement to the
inhabitants of both towns.'*

The Germans initially tried to get the civilian doctors to inspect
the brothels twice a week, but later they had to get their own
MOs to do the job as the civilian doctors were far too busy
looking after their own patients.

Fraternisation

Human nature being what it is, there were inevitably some
cases of German servicemen fraternising with local women. For
some it was a case of true love, as is evidenced by those who

Inevitably there was some fraternisation as was the case in every occupied country of Europe, but it was extremely limited on the islands. Société Jersiaise

returned to the Islands once they had been released from POW camp, to marry their wartime sweethearts. As Leslie Sinel sensibly puts it in his taped ineterview:

> *'You've got to remember that the girls were in their teens, they wanted things and they were attracted by the Germans – and some of the young Germans were quite likeable, especially those who worked on a farm and could get to know some girls in the district. They are to be condemned but it was a natural thing that happened in every place where there were occupying forces. That's the sort of thing you expect.'*

Air warfare

After the intense activity of the Battle of Britain there was still a significant amount of air warfare over the islands, but it did not assume major proportions until the Normandy invasion in June 1944. However, from time to time there were raids by the RAF on the ports (eg: on St Peter Port in January 1942) and on shipping at sea, as the Allies tried to reduce the amount of sea traffic between the Islands and France. Inevitably this led to civilian supply ships being sunk, some of which contained innocent OT workers and POWs. One local historian quotes that there were at least 22 raids on the Channel Islands, between 1940-45, which resulted in 93 deaths and 250 injuries – many being OT port workers caught whilst at work or enroute between France and the Islands.[1] Inevitably also, aircraft were shot down and the pilots ended up on the Islands, either, sadly, as corpses washed in on the beaches, or alive,when they were normally captured by the Germans, despite civilian efforts to hide them. More of this and similar naval casualties later, however, here I want to use air warfare as a lead-in to describing one of the most significant parts of the garrison, being at its height in total a complete anti-aircraft brigade. Initially this was *Flakbrigade* XII, which had its headquarters on Guernsey and comprised two regiments: *Flakregiment* 39 in Guernsey and *Flakregiment* 40 in Jersey. Both heavy AA guns, such as the 8.8cm Flak 41 and lighter guns – the 2cm Flak 38 and the 3.7cm Flak 18, were in service, there being more 8.8cm Flak guns on the Islands than on any other part of the Atlantic Wall, namely six batteries in both Jersey and Guernsey, plus a further three in Alderney, making a total of 15 batteries with 90 guns in all.

Flak Gunners

Anti-aircraft (AA) gunners were of course members of the *Luftwaffe* rather than the *Heer*, and life in a Flak battery was the usual mixture of short periods of activity and long periods of boredom. Dieter Hankel was a platoon commander, then the

By 1942 much of the air activity was army co-operation work between the islands and the mainland, using the remarkable Fieseler Storch Fi 156, which could could take off in 60m and land in about 20m. Hans Gerhard Sandmann

A 2cm Flak 38 gun in what appears to be a wooden firing position. The Luftwaffe had numerous batteries of various types of AA guns (ranging from 2cm up to 8.8cm) on the islands – making up a complete Flak brigade. They were amongst the busiest elements of the garrison. Guernsey Museum

battery commander of the 8th Mixed Battery of 292 AA Battalion (8./*Gemischt Flakabteilung* 292) on Guernsey in a position on the west side of Perelle Bay. Each of the four platoons in the battery comprised 3 x 2cm Flak 38, two machine guns and various small arms. He had arrived to find that his defensive position left a lot to be desired. His tasks were twofold: to repulse air attacks especially from low flying aircraft, and also attacks from the sea. He was worried because he had no safe shelter for ammunition, equipment and spare parts, except for two 'very obvious' small houses which was where they had their quarters and the platoon office.

'We were on show', he wrote later, *'and a single heavy naval shell or a small bomb could have blown us into the air and would have put a quick end to our defence position.' Rumours of British commando raids added to his worries and he envisaged them '... coming in at low tide, wearing dark overalls and with blackened faces. Now I get a funny feeling in the pit of my stomach!' he commented. He discussed the matter with others in the battery and then put in a demand for additional weapons, such as an anti-tankgun, and better fortifications, steel obstacles and barbed wire, together with an OT labour squad to help his soldiers to build a defensive trench system which he had designed. He sent his demands up through "official channels" but heard no more*

until he was unexpectedly visited by some staff officers. "I used all my powers of persuasion, but they were only willing to grant part of my demands. Most of all they denied the need for a bunker with an anti-tank gun and one of them said that it should be possible for me to get one of my AA guns and anti-tank ammunition transported down to the roadside in time for me to meet a seaborne attack. That was enough! In correct military posture I said: "Sir, I could do so if the English announced an intended attack beforehand." The officers seemed offended and left my base without a word of goodbye. I immediately informed my CO and he gave me a severe dressing down because of my answer.'

Despite his 'rocket' Dieter's CO personally backed him up and in time the general himself came to inspect his base, accompanied by a small number of senior officers and staff. After only an hour, everything was granted, and a week later work began:

'After three months my position was finished to a sufficient extent to enable us to defend it to the best of our ability.'[2]

Another Flak gunner was *Feldwebel* Josef H Gerhaher who was in the same battalion as Dieter Hankel but in a different batteries and served first with 1st Battery at Castle Cornet, then at Battalion HQ at St Martin's and finally with the 9th Battery at Fort George. He told me:

'The daily life was normally fairly quiet, but from time to time there were air raid alarms, mostly without attacks. However, in my diary I found the following listed:

Off duty anti-aircraft gunners play cards in their snug bunker, with a portrait of their Fuehrer above the door. Guernsey Museum

31 Dec 43 – *two planes shot down*

07 Jan 44 – *one Thunderbolt shot down*

27 May 44 – *two Thunderbolts shot down during an air raid on Fort George Freya Wuerzburg Riese Goldfisch radar. No damage.*

28 May 44 – *ditto*

05 Jun 44 – *three planes shot down*

18 Jun 44 – *one plane shot down during a raid on St Peter Port harbour*

28 Feb 45 – *two planes shot down during a raid on Fort George radar'*

These are significant results for one battery, however, comparing these figures with the actual day-to-day casualty figures in official RAF records is difficult, but then AA gunners are invariably born optimists! He continues:

'An average day comprised normal military duties such as watch, training, lessons of various kinds, all carried out under the continual pressure of everlasting readiness, being ready to fight with the enemy at any time. Also, our gun crews were smaller than normal, so free time was rare.'

The Mirus Battery

During 1942, the massive fortifications began to take shape and the artillery guns installed. We will examine them more closely 'in the round' during the next chapter, as 1943 was perhaps the mid-point of all the building programmes. However, it would be wrong not to mention that in 1942, a remarkable event took place in that in April the first of the massive guns of Batterie Mirus was test-fired. This was by far the heaviest of all the coastal batteries, consisting of four 30.5cm naval guns, located on the high ground at St Saviour's Guernsey.

The battery comprised four reconditioned Russian guns which had once been part of the main armament of the Tsar's 22,600 ton Imperial Russian Navy battleship *Imperator Alexandr Troti* (later renamed *Volya* (Victory) when with the White Russian Fleet). The guns had been manufactured by the Russian Putilov Arsenal in 1914. When the battleship was eventually broken up in a French Tunisian dockyard in 1935, the twelve usable guns were put into storage, then in the winter of 1939/40 given to Finland, to help them in their war against the USSR.

Ramming one of the enormous shells into the breech of the 12inch gun took teamwork by its large crew. (IWM - HU 29064)

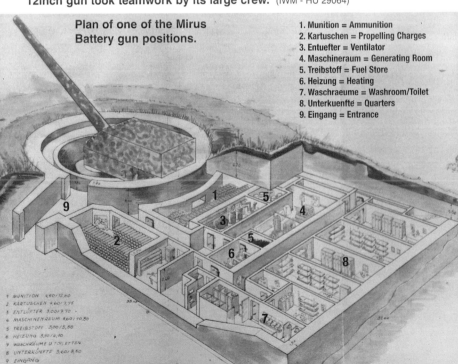

Plan of one of the Mirus Battery gun positions.

1. Munition = Ammunition
2. Kartuschen = Propelling Charges
3. Entuefter = Ventilator
4. Maschinenraum = Generating Room
5. Treibstoff = Fuel Store
6. Heizung = Heating
7. Waschraeume = Washroom/Toilet
8. Unterkuenfte = Quarters
9. Eingang = Entrance

1 MUNITION 4,80/12,60
2 KARTUSCHEN 4,60/2,75
3 ENTLÜFTER 3,00/2,70
4 MASCHINENRAUM 4,60/10,50
5 TREIBSTOFF 3,00/3,80
6 HEIZUNG 3,50/2,10
7 WASCHRÄUME U TOILETTEN
8 UNTERKÜNFTE 3,60/8,50
9 EINGANG

The guns were put onto three ships (four guns each) and shipped to Finland, however, one of the ships was delayed en route and subsequently captured by the Germans when they invaded Norway in May 1940. When heavy coastal guns were needed for the Atlantic Wall, someone remembered the four guns (then in storage in Bergen, Norway) and they were taken to the Krupps works in the Ruhr and reconditioned. Then began their journey from St Malo, by sea, to Guernsey, a special floating crane having to be brought to St Peter Port to unload them. This was followed by a tortuous road journey on a twenty-four-wheel trailer, towed by four large half-tracks (probably the Mercedes Benz 12 ton SdKfz8), for which some of the roads had to be specially widened in places in order to get round the bends.

The enormous 12 inch guns had a range of twenty-six miles, some six miles less than the original maximum range, because firing trials had shown that reduced charges would have to be used on the vintage guns, indeed the normal working range was deliberately limited to twenty miles. In German parlance the guns were known as the 30.5cm K(E)626(r) or just K14(r). The first gun was eventually test-fired on 13 April 1942 and by August all four guns were operational, the event being

This recent photograph of one of the Mirus gun pits, shows just how massive each position was. Brian Matthews

celebrated by an article in the *Deutsche Guernsey Zeitung* on 12 August 42, under the banner 'Woe to the English!'. What the article did not do was to explain that eighteen months plus work had gone on to complete the project, seriously delaying all other construction work on the island. The figures are staggering – 47,000 cubic metres of concrete had to be poured into the four massive gun emplacements, each with associated personnel shelters, radar mountings, anti-aircraft bunkers, etc. The fire direction centre comprised three separate installations: a command centre and crew quarters; a radar location; and a rangefinder bunker. All were made of reinforced concrete and the rangefinder was connected to the command centre by a long underground tunnel. Despite their potential firepower it has been estimated that the guns only fired about seventy rounds each, mostly on training and false alarms. On one night for example, suspicious 'blips' on the radar were interpreted as an enemy landing force, causing the acting SEEKO-KI *Oberstleutenant* Pedell (SEEKO-KI proper was away visiting Alderney) to panic and order the battery to open fire together with other coastal artillery. When daylight came the 'enemy' were found to be two half-submerged British barrage balloons.

Deportations

As stated earlier, the claim about the deportation of male civilians was perfectly true, indeed the sad saga of deportations had begun much earlier when action was taken against those Jews who had not left the islands before the occupation began. Some were certainly deported, others 'vanished', so the story is incomplete and their fate not properly recorded, although at least one source claims to have seen a letter recommending their deportation to Dachau.

The decision to deport those of English birth is certainly better documented, and this 'pogrom' began in September 1941, when

---

Feldkommandantur 515.
Jersey, den 15. September 1942.

NOTICE

By order of higher authorities the following British Subjects will be evacuated and transferred to Germany :

a) Persons who have their permanent residence not on the Channel Islands, for instance, those who have been caught here by the outbreak of the war,

b) all those men not born on the Channel Islands and 16 to 70 years of age who belong o the English people, together with their families.

Detailed instructions will be given by the Feldkommandantur 515.

Der Feldkommandant :

KNACKFUSS,
Oberst.

95

Hitler personally ordered lists to be provided, initially of those English government officials who were living in Jersey on a British pension. After some stalling, figures were grudgingly produced – there were some 180 of which one was a distant relative of mine, Lieutenant Colonel (Retd) Heber Forty, but more of him later. Other lists were then demanded, by age groups and covering all the islands, including details of UK born women and children. By early November the lists were completed to the satisfaction of the *Feldkommandantur*, covering over 2,000 unfortunates. A warning was then passed that if the British interned German citizens in Persia, then the British citizens would be treated likewise. To cut a long story short, despite strong arguments that the potential deportees could be of more use to the Germans if they stayed on the islands (eg: as labour, helping to build fortifications, and as a deterrent against British attacks being mounted), deportations did take place in September 1942, and after many setbacks, permanent accomodation was eventually provided for them in camps at Birberach, Wuerzach and Laufen, where the majority had to wait until they were liberated by the advancing Allied armies.

My relative, who, during his army service had worked for the King of Siam, was clearly a man of considerable initiative. Not only did he successfuly prevent the Germans from taking over his house, but also demanded – and got back – a smooth-bore gun which HM King Rama had personally presented to him and which they had confiscated. Clearly such a determined character would not allow himself to be deported and when told by the authorities that his name was on the list, he 'acquired' some sheets of the local doctor's writing paper, forged a medical certificate complete with the doctor's signature, saying that he was much too ill to travel – and got away with it.

Notes

1. See Peter King: *The Channel Islands War 1940-45* page 22

2. Extracted from an article by Dieter Hankel in the *Channel Islands Occupation Review* No 24 and appears here with kind permission of CIOS Guernsey

Chapter Six

1943 – CONTINUED GROWTH

Full to bursting

By May 1943, the total strength of the *Wehrmacht* was 26,800 (Guernsey, 13,000; Jersey, 10,000; Alderney, 3,800), whilst that of the Organization Todt was 16,000, giving a combined total of 42,800. This was to be the largest concentration ever, being equivalent to over two-thirds of the total civilian population that had remained on the Islands. Thereafter numbers would drop slightly, but there would still be 23,700 *Wehrmacht* there at the end of the year and much the same numbers after D Day the following June.

Naval Artillery

In addition to the normal responsibilities for naval activities via the three Harbour Commanders (*Hafenkommandanten*) at St Peter Port (Guernsey), St Helier (Jersey) and St Anne (Alderney), SEEKO-KI's most important function was for the actual defence of the Islands via the naval and coastal artillery. As we have seen, the sea traffic was considerable from the outset (troop movements, supplies, leave parties, deportations,

Castle Cornet, on the southern breakwater of St Peter Port, Guernsey in 1943, being viewed from another part of the old harbour by a German soldier. Werener Wagenknecht

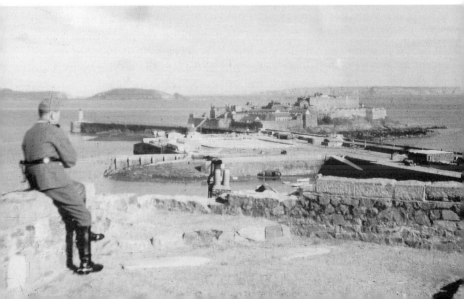

This 22cm gun belonged to Batterie Strassburg which was No 1 Battery of Marine Artillerie Abteilung 604 (MAA 604) stationed at Jerbourg Point, Guernsey. The 22cm K 532(f) gun was French in origin and was photographed during a high-powered visit in July 1941. MAA 604 and MAA 605 had begun to arrive in May 1941, but were not complete for quite a long time. CIOS Jersey

etc) but this increased dramatically with the decision to fortify the islands. Considerable extra harbour machinery had to be brought in – an outstanding example being a large French-built, Dutch-owned floating derrick, the *Antee*, which arrived in Guernsey in late 1941. Its first job was, as explained already, to unload the massive gun barrels for the Batterie Mirus. As mentioned at the start of the last chapter, Hitler's Directive No 40 of 23 March 1942, put responsibility for preventing enemy landings squarely onto the *Kriegsmarine,* so it became one of SEEKO-KI primary tasks and gave him the authority to fire a wide range of coastal artillery guns. These included:

a. Marine Artillerie Abteilung (MAA) 604 &605. These two Naval Artillery battalions operated coastal artillery batteries MA 604 on Jersey and Guernsey, MAA 605 on Alderney, being spread as follows:

MAA 604 – HQ and Staff – St Martin's Guernsey

No1 Bty (*Strassburg Batterie*) – Jerbourg Point, Guernsey – 4 x

22cm K 532(f) guns

No2 Bty (*Steinbruch Batterie*) – Les Vardes, Guernsey – 4 x 15cm SK c/28 guns

No3 Bty (*Lothringen Batterie*) – Noirmont Point, Jersey – 4 x 15cm SK L/45 guns

Mirus Batterie – Le Frie Baton, Guernsey – 4 x 30.5cm K 626(r)

Sark Batterie – Little Sark – 3 x 8.8cm SK guns (taken from a laid up naval vessel in Oct '44)

MAA 605 – HQ & Staff – Alderney (from June 1942)

No 1 Bty (*Elsass Batterie*) – Fort Albert, Alderney – 3 x 17cm SK L/40

No2 Bty (*Annes Batterie*) – West Coast, Alderney – 4 x 15cm SK c/28

No3 Bty (*Marcks Batterie*) – Western slopes of Fort Albert – 4 x 10.5cm K331(f) – from June '44

Each battery had first to operate in temporary positions, but later concrete platforms were added, then crew bunkers and ammunition shelters. Also, in order to provide close protection for these large coastal guns, a wide range of smaller weapons (field guns, AA guns, anti-tank guns, machine guns and mortars) plus searchlights were supplied. Initially MAA 604 had to cover Alderney, batteries changing on a roster basis. However this produced considerable upheaval and affected the operational capabilities of batteries whilst they were changing over. It was rectified in June 1942, with the arrival of MAA 605 which took over Alderney completely and their CO became ARKO Alderney.

Leitstande

All these naval coastal batteries had command posts (CPs) (*Leitstande*) in well-constructed bunkers, equipped like the CPs of up to date warships. One such command post remains virtually intact at Noirmont Point, Jersey. They were connected to the naval direction and rangefinding towers *Marinenpeilstanede* which are listed later.

b.Heeres Kuesten Artillerie Regiment 1265 (HKAR 1265). The various army coastal artillery units which had arrived piecemeal, were in May 1943, formed into a coastal artillery regiment HKAR 1265, with its HQ at 'Tannenburg', Oberlands Road, Guernsey, the CO being ARKO Guernsey. There were four battalions in the regiment, two on Jersey (I & II) and two on Guernsey and Alderney (III & IV) with their sixteen batteries located as follows:

JERSEY
Batterie Endrass – 4 x 10.5cm K 331(f) field guns, at Westmount, St Helier (task was to block entry to the harbour).
Batterie Schliefen and Batterie Haeseler – both 4 x 15cm K18 medium field guns, located at Verclut, Grouville and La Coupe, St Martin.
Batterie Moltke – 4 x 15cm K 418(f) heavy field guns, at Les Landes, St Ouen.
Batterie Ludendorff, Batterie Hindenburg & Batterie Mackensen – all 3 x 21cm Moerser 18 field howitzers near to St Ouen's Church, Route Orange St Brelade and St Martin's Church.
Batterie Roon – 4 x 22cm K532(f) heavy field guns, at La Moye Point, St Brelade.

GUERNSEY & ALDERNEY
Batterie Naumannshohe – 4 x 10.5cm K331(f) field guns, at Cambridge Park, St Peter Port.
Batterie Bluecher – 4 x 15cm K18 medium field guns at St Anne, Alderney.
Batterie Barbara – 4 x 15.5cm K418(f) heavy field guns, at North View.
Batterie Elefant, Batterie Mammut and **Batterie Rhinozeros** all 3 x 21cm Moerser 18 field howitzers, at La Chaumiere, Les Effards and Beauchamps respectively, all at Catel.
Batterie Dollmann & **Batterie Radetsky** – each 4 x 22cm K532(f) heavy field guns, at Pleinmont Point and L'Eree.

Fire control
Despite these guns being army manned and under command of the various island ARKOs, it was the naval SEEKO-KI who had the ultimate responsibility for coastal defence, so the Army and Navy units involved in coastal defence had to work closely together to fulfil their tasks which were:

a. to prevent landings on the Channel Islands

b. to protect all German shipping moving between the Islands and between the Islands and France.

c. to protect naval vessels using the core route between Cherbourg and Brest

d. to protect the Gulf of St Malo

SEEKO-KI also had responsibility over the parts of *Artillerie Regiment 319*, which manned coastal guns and beach bunkers, whilst even the *Luftwaffe* Flak guns had an element of control from him, although AA guns could fire at enemy aircraft without first getting his approval.

Observation Towers

If one examines all parts of the Atlantic Wall, then one will find a commonality in the types of bunkers built, because the weapons and equipment which were installed, despite their differing countries of origin, were all roughly similar. However, only on the Channel Islands did they design and build such an amazing array of tall, reinforced concrete observation towers – a staggering twenty-two of which were planned although only nine were eventually built. Of the nine built, seven are still standing, so they remain as prime examples of the German defences. The futuristic towers have a series of observation slots facing out to sea – on the average this was five on the Islands, whereas the 'norm' for the rest of the Wall was just two. The reason for the multiplicity of observation slots in these *Marinenpeilstaende* (naval direction and range finding towers) was that each slot dealt with a single coastal battery, making control much easier. A full list of the towers is given over the page (including those that can still be seen):

Marinenpeilstaende MP4 was built at L'Angle, near Pleinmont, Guernsey, was one of the largest direction finding towers built on the islands. It was of unique design, but still served the same purpose, with each floor providing observation for a separate coastal artillery battery.
IWM - HU 29143

MP	Location	Remarks
JERSEY		
1	Noirmont Point	Complete and open to the public
2	La Corbiere	Completed (now used by Jersey Radio, to monitor shipping)
3	Les Landes	Completed (very impressive)
4	Plémont	Not built
5	Sorel Point	ditto
6	Belle Hougue Point	ditto
7	La Coupe, St Martin	ditto
8	Mont Mallet, St Martin	ditto
9	Rue de la Hougette	ditto
GUERNSEY		
1	Chouet headland	Completed but now demolished due to subsidence
2	Fort Saumerez	Completed (joined to a Martello Tower)
3	Pleinmont	Completed and now restored
4	L'Angle	Completed
5	La Prevote	Not built
6	Vale Mill	completed as an Army coastal OP, now partly destroyed
7	Icart Point	Not built
8	Jerbourg Point	ditto
ALDERNEY		
1	Telegraph Bay	Not built
2	SW of Essex Castle	ditto
3	Mannez	Completed
4	Fort Albert headland	Not built
5	Fort Tourgis	ditto
6	La Giffoine	ditto

TOTALS

Proposed   **22**
Built   **9**
Still Standing   **7** (but Vale Mill is partly demolished)

Other naval tasks

Of course SEEKO-KI had other purely naval responsibilities which were just as important and included:-

a. **Harbour Defence Flotillas** (*hafenschutzflotillen*), these comprised small armed boats, primarily for harbour defence duties in St Peter Port and St Helier, however after D Day they did take part in other activities.

b. *Matrosenkompanien 'Koenig' und 'Hilger'* – These two special naval infantry companies were based in Jersey and Guernsey respectively, where they took over the manning of most of the infantry strongpoints in the St Aubin's Bay area and from St Peter Port to St Sampson.

c. *Schnellboote* (E-Boats) – None were stationed in the Islands for

The Crown Hotel, St Peter Port, Guernsey was the German Naval HQ. It is now the Royal Channel Islands Yacht Club.
Hans-Gerhard Sandmann

long periods as they normally operated out of Cherbourg, where the 5th and 6th Flotillas were based. However, from time to time they would locate in Guernsey to carry out raids, or call in on their way to/from their main bases.

d. *Minensuchflottillen* – From D Day onwards Minesweeping Flotillas 24 and 46 were virtually trapped on the

Excellent photograph of three minesweepers of the 24th Minensuchflottillen (Minesweeping Flotilla), which comprised nine vessels in all and was virtually trapped on the islands after D Day. Converted fishing vessels were also used for mine sweeping
CIOS Jersey

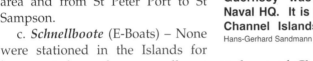

islands. Most were a variety of fishing boats adapted for mine sweeping and laying

e. **Submarines** – Like the E Boats, there were no submarines permanently stationed in the Islands, but they did visit from time to time to berth up and refuel. U275 was in St Peter Port during the early hours of 14 Jun 44, when it was attacked by American P-47 Thunderbolts. They missed with their rockets but struck a ship berthed opposite (the MV *Karel*, a Dutch registered motor vessel which was being used to ferry supplies from France for the garrison). There was a plan to build an underground fuel store near St Peter Port harbour because the Germans were experiencing problems with the RAF bombing the fuel tanks adjacent to Castle Cornet (U boats were to be refuelled in the bay behind the Aquarium tunnel and fuel pumped through to them at their moorings). However, the complex was never completed and is now the site of the La Valette Underground Military Museum, where one of the massive fuel tanks can still be seen.

f. *Artillerietraeger.* *Kriegsmarine* 'Floating artillery' carriers which normally carried artillery, but were used for a number of other tasks which included escort duties, minelaying, troop car-

Motor Vessel Robert Mueller 8 was just one of many supply ships operating between the French coast and the Channel Islands. It operated with its original German civilian crew, plus AA specialists to man its guns. Amongst its many cargoes were the deportees. CIOS Jersey

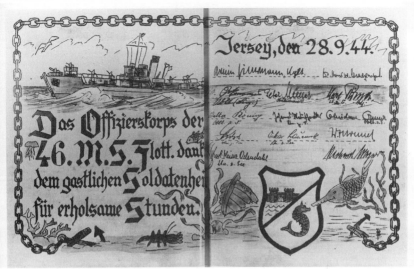

Auf Wiedersehen Guernsey! When 46th Minesweeping Flotilla eventually left in September 1944, they inscribed the Guest Book at the St Brelade's Bay Hotel. Robert Colley

rying and even as landing barges, was another way of boosting artillery cover for convoys. Eventually there were just three artillery carriers (AF65, AF68 and AF71) operating, two out of Guernsey and one Jersey.

g. **Merchant shipping** – Of course all sorts of ships were used to bring the food, ammunition, war supplies, etc, for both the garrision and the civilian population, including ships from German, French, Dutch and various other continental countries, plus those belonging to the Islands. Some had crews of German merchant seamen, others still had their original crews. Invariably German light AA guns and other weapons were added for protection purposes as all were fair game to the Allies and were regularly attacked. Sadly this led to the deaths of numerous innocent victims, in particular slave labourers. However, the Islands could not have been maintained as a fortress without this life-line, as was graphically illustrated during the 'Hunger Winter' of 1944/45.

German Naval Signal Headquarters

Radio communications were a vital part of operations at SEEKO-KI headquarters and initially powerful radio transmitters and receivers were housed in the loft of La Collinette and La Porte Hotels, where HQ SEEKO-KI had been established in the summer of 1942. However, in the autumn of

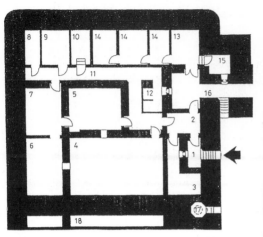

The layout of the German Naval Signals Bunker.

1. Entrance
2. Gaslock
3. Entrance defence
4. Operations Room
5. Signal Officer's Room
6. Transmitters
7. Teletype Room
8. Officers' Bedroom
9. Ventilation
10. Boiler Room
11. Corridor
12. Toilets and Washroom
13. Radio Room
14. Stores/Fuel
15. Entrance Defence
16. Tunnel to Signals HQ
17. Observation Post
18. Antennae

Naval Signal Headquarters. Good reliable communications were essential, so HQ SEEKO-KI established a permanent bunker in the grounds of the La Collinette Hotel, which has been fully restored. Brian Green via Fortress Guernsey

Plan of St Helier and surrounding area. Courtesy Howard B Baker

ARMAMENTS

VISIONAL ARTILLERY BATTERIES CLASSIFICATION

Field guns in semi-permanent positions.

Light howitzers in semi-permanent positions.

ANTI-AIRCRAFT BATTERIES CLASSIFICATION

Guns in semi-permanent positions.

Guns in permanent positions.

Guns in "fortress" positions.

BATTLE HEADQUARTERS

Fortress Commander's bunker H.Q.

Artillery Regiment 319 bunker H.Q.

Infantry Regiment 582 bunker H.Q.

HEADQUARTERS

REGULAR BATTALION HEADQUARTERS, ARTILLERY AND INFANTRY

HQ Battalion 364 Anti-Aircraft Regiment 49

Battalion H.Q.'s for Infantry Regiment 582

H.Q.'s of Divisional Artillery Battalions 319 Regiment

H.Q.'s of Coastal Artillery Battalions 1265 Regiment

H.Q. of 3rd Battery Naval Artillery Battalion 604.

MISCELLANEOUS HEADQUARTERS

Details indicated on map.

MISCELLANEOUS

Land — Reinforced concrete anti-tank wall.

Coast — Anti-tank ditch

Defence Sector boundary NB These extended out to sea

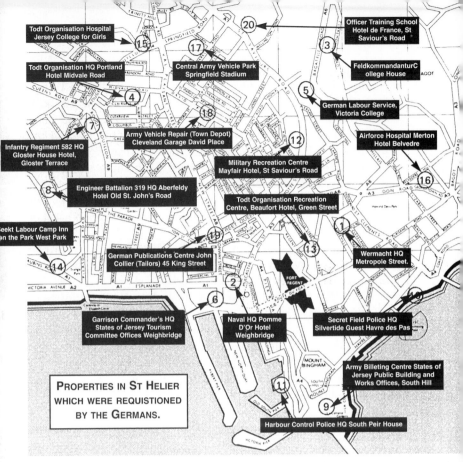

Map labels:

- Todt Organisation Hospital Jersey College for Girls — 15
- Officer Training School Hotel de France, St Saviour's Road — 3
- 20
- 17
- Todt Organisation HQ Portland Hotel Midvale Road — 4
- Central Army Vehicle Park Springfield Stadium
- FeldkommandanturC ollege House
- German Labour Service, Victoria College — 5
- 18
- Army Vehicle Repair (Town Depot) Cleveland Garage David Place
- 7
- Airforce Hospital Merton Hotel Belvedre
- Infantry Regiment 582 HQ Gloster House Hotel, Gloster Terrace
- 12
- Military Recreation Centre Mayfair Hotel, St Saviour's Road
- 16
- Engineer Battalion 319 HQ Aberfeldy Hotel Old St. John's Road
- 8
- Todt Organisation Recreation Centre, Beaufort Hotel, Green Street
- 1
- Seekt Labour Camp Inn on the Park West Park
- 19
- German Publications Centre John Collier (Tailors) 45 King Street
- 13
- Wermacht HQ Metropole Street.
- 14
- 2
- 6
- Garrison Commander's HQ States of Jersey Tourism Committee Offices Weighbridge
- Naval HQ Pomme D'Or Hotel Weighbridge
- Secret Field Police HQ Silvertide Guest Havre des Pas
- Army Billeting Centre States of Jersey Public Building and Works Offices, South Hill
- 11
- 9
- Harbour Control Police HQ South Peir House

PROPERTIES IN ST HELIER WHICH WERE REQUISITIONED BY THE GERMANS.

1943 it was decided to build a permanent bunker in the grounds of La Collinette Hotel, which was in full operation by 1 February 1944. It then handled all the important radio signals traffic for German forces in the Islands and became even more important after the Islands were isolated by the Normandy landings. Messages were sent and received using the Enigma enciphering machines, the bulk of the traffic going, first to the Naval HQ in Paris, then during the final months of the war, direct to Berlin. The Signals Headquarters bunker has been restored by members of the CIOS (Guernsey) in co-operation with Fortress Guernsey and is open to the public.

Operation TUNNEL

On the night of 23/24 October 1943, six Royal Navy destroyers, together with the light cruiser HMS *Charybdis* were carrying our a sweep west of the Channel Islands and out of range of the coastal batteries. They were hoping to surprise enemy merchantmen, however, unfortunately it was the British force that was surprised by a group of E boats, which had been warned by a shore radar station. Before the cruiser could open fire she was struck by two torpedoes and sunk, as was the destroyer HMS *Limbourne*. Between the two vessels a total of 31 officers and 473 ratings lost their lives, 51 being washed upon the Islands – 21 on Guernsey, 29 on Jersey and one on Sark. On Guernsey they were buried with a full *Kriegsmarine* honour guard and over five thousand islanders, in a spontaneous act of loyalty to Great Britain, turned out to pay their respects at Foulon Cemetery, Guernsey. Afterwards the subsequent British board of enquiry was severely critical saying that the force was: 'ill-assorted, unwieldly and untrained.'

Nevertheless, both the Royal Navy and the RAF continued to attack enemy shipping, which added to the continuous deterioration in the effectiveness of convoys to and from mainland France. In 1943 it became so bad that, because the *Luftwaffe* could not provide the fighter aircraft to deal with Allied air attacks, there was a complete ban on the movement of ships by day.

Inspection of the defences

In November 1943, *Vizeadmiral* Friedrich Rieve, the admiral commanding the Channel coast (*Kommandierender Admiral Kanalkueste*) visited the Islands to inspect the defences but did not find everything to his liking. He was, however, able to see the guns in a real action when six Allied bombers attacked shipping in St Peter Port. He also visited Batterie Mirus, and was pleased with the way the mock farm buildings had helped to camouflage the site. However, he commented that the Batterie Elsass on Alderney and Batterie Strassburg on Guernsey were short of equipment, whilst Batterie Steinbruch, also on Guernsey needed camouflaging. He recommended the planting of some hedges and the erection of dummy greenhouses, and, most importantly, the dismantling of the Doyle Monument, just nearby, which was a perfect landmark for attacking bombers. Other batteries needed more protection, and Batterie Lothringen on Jersey, was badly camouflaged and its ammunition store was unprotected. He also commented upon the state of the troops and was satisfied with their standard, except for the new arrivals – those between 47-49, having 'broken bodies and little enthusiasm ... the last reserves of the Wehrmacht'. He felt that they would probably all end up 'filling the hospitals' which would have a bad effect on the morale of the others. Transport arrangements between the mainland and the Islands also came in for criticism. Granted, the bad weather and difficult navigation were unavoidable, but the lack of transports was most unsatisfactory. Currently some 300 soldier passengers had to stand on deck throughout the six hour journey, so at least two fast troop transports were urgently required. The postal service was also far too slow, taking up to twelve days for letters to and from Germany, which was bad for morale. He also commented on the poor state of the harbour protection flotillas.

Rieve's report was greatly at variance with the more glossy propaganda of the war correspondents ('manufactured' by Goebbels propaganda machine) in their articles for home consumption, one of which is quoted by Charles Cruickshank in his book: *The German Occupation of the Channel Islands*:

> *'An army of OT workers has been for years working alongside the soldiers of the Wehrmacht and is still busy building fortifications ... Hundreds of thousands of cubic metres of concrete now protect the coasts, many more will follow ... dense minefields and long anti-tank walls hermetically seal the beaches. German soldiers, tried in battle, man our best weapons and form a ring of steel around these former British possessions, which lie like anchored fortresses in the Atlantic Wall.'*

DEATH CAMPS ON ALDERNEY

Meanwhile the situation for the OT workers on Alderney in particular, had grown steadily worse, especially for the poor unfortunate Russian slave labourers who were working to build some of the vast number of fortications that had been planned for the island. A British Intelligence officer, the late Major 'Bunny' Pantcheff, who had spent time on the island before the war, was sent in May 1945 to carry out a detailed inquiry into what had happened there during the German occupation. Subsequently he retired to the island and wrote a book: *Alderney – Fortress Island* in which he chronicles all that went on between

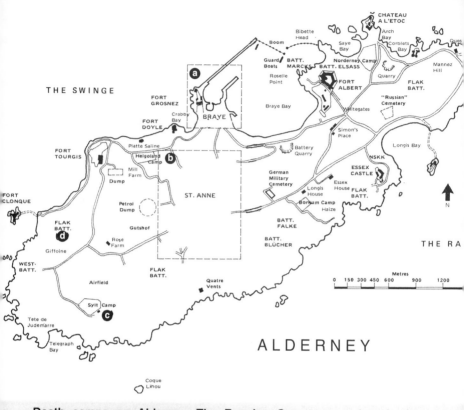

The map shows various locations on Alderney including: THE SWINGE, FORT GROSNEZ, FORT DOYLE, Crabby Bay, Platte Saline, FORT TOURGIS, Mill Farm, Dump, FORT CLONQUE, FLAK BATT. (d), Giffoine, WEST-BATT., Airfield, Petrol Dump, Gutshof, Rose Farm, ST. ANNE, BRAYE, Helgoland Camp (b), Sylt Camp (c), Tete de Judemarre, Telegraph Bay, Coque Lihou, FLAK BATT., Quatre Vents, BATT. BLÜCHER, BATT. FALKE, German Military Cemetery, Longis House, Borkum Camp Haize, Essex House, ESSEX CASTLE, FLAK BATT., NSKK, Longis Bay, "Russian" Cemetery, Simon's Place, Whitegates, Battery Quarry, Braye Bay, Roselle Point, Guard Boats, BATT. MARCKS, BATT. ELSASS, Norderney Camp, FORT ALBERT, Saye Bay, Bibette Head, Boom, CHATEAU A L'ETOC, Arch Bay, Corblets Bay, Ques, Mannez Hill, FLAK BATT., Quarry, THE RA[CE], ALDERNEY

Scale: Metres 0 150 300 450 600 900 1200
N (north arrow)

Death camps on Alderney. The Russian Cemetery on Longis Common, Alderney, where murdered slave labourers were buried, in: 'repulsive conditions' to quote a German source. The photograph was taken in 1945, but in 1963 they were all exhumed and reburied in Normandy. Alderney Society and Museum

26 February 1942 when the slave workers arrived and 22 June 1944 when they were withdrawn to the mainland, listing 389 confirmed deaths amongst those on Alderney.

The workforce was put into four camps (wooden hutted and fence with barbed wire), with names of islands in the North Sea, which had been built between January and June 1942 by a force of volunteer, paid, Belgian workers. These camps were:

a. **Helgoland or No 1 Camp** – Built on the south side of a new concrete road constructed by the Germans in the Platte Saline beach area. It housed up to 1,500 slave labourers, principally Russians.

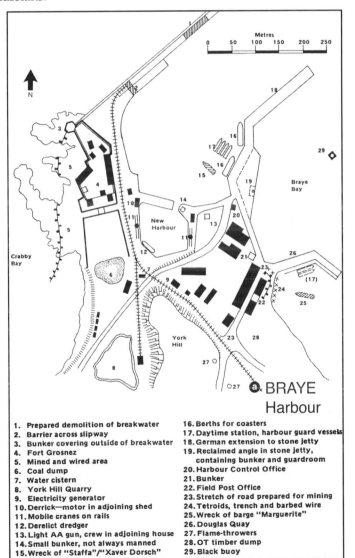

1. Prepared demolition of breakwater
2. Barrier across slipway
3. Bunker covering outside of breakwater
4. Fort Grosnez
5. Mined and wired area
6. Coal dump
7. Water cistern
8. York Hill Quarry
9. Electricity generator
10. Derrick—motor in adjoining shed
11. Mobile cranes on rails
12. Derelict dredger
13. Light AA gun, crew in adjoining house
14. Small bunker, not always manned
15. Wreck of "Staffa"/"Xaver Dorsch"
16. Berths for coasters
17. Daytime station, harbour guard vessels
18. German extension to stone jetty
19. Reclaimed angle in stone jetty, containing bunker and guardroom
20. Harbour Control Office
21. Bunker
22. Field Post Office
23. Stretch of road prepared for mining
24. Tetroids, trench and barbed wire
25. Wreck of barge "Marguerite"
26. Douglas Quay
27. Flame-throwers
28. OT timber dump
29. Black buoy

b. **Nordeney or No 2 Camp** – Built on the low ground between Saye Farm and Chateau a L'Etoc. It housed a mixture of Russian and European slave workers, together with some German volunteers and had a capacity of about 1,500. It was taken over by the SS in February 1944.

1. Connaught Square
2. Island Commandant's HQ
3. Soldatenheim
4. Observation tower
5. Mouriaux House
6. Moroccan PW billets
7. Flak HQ and workshops (Grand Hotel and Butes Arsenal)
8. Bakery
9. Food store (Methodist Chapel)
10. Petrol dump
11. Military Hospital
12. Communal kitchen
13. Val des Portes mess
14. Parish Church and churchyard
15. Court House building
16. Pay Office
17. Out-station HQ of FK 515
18. Billeting office and store (Militia Arsenal)
19. Slaughterhouse
20. Underground storage dump
21. Coal dump
22. Carpenter's shop
23. Furniture store
24. Military police (Jubilee Home)
25. Cinema
26. "Hoffmannshöhe" — tactical HQ
27. Naval operational HQ and communications centre

c. **Bokum or No 3 Camp** – Built behind Logis House it was used to house German and volunteer specialist craftsmen, with numbers between 500 and 1,000.

d. **Sylt of No 4 Camp** – Built south of the airfield, it could hold up to 1,000 and was used initially by the OT for Russian and other slave labour, but was then handed over to the SS in March 1943.

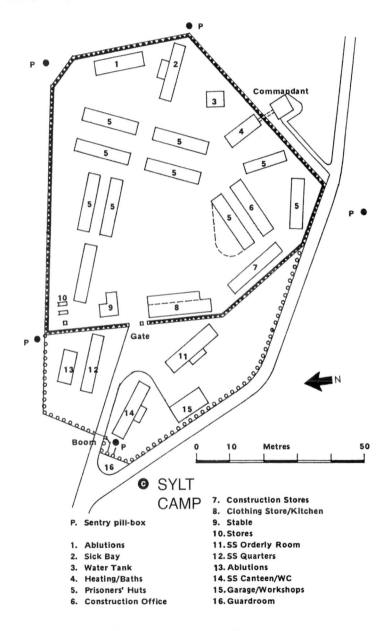

SYLT CAMP

P. Sentry pill-box

1. Ablutions
2. Sick Bay
3. Water Tank
4. Heating/Baths
5. Prisoners' Huts
6. Construction Office
7. Construction Stores
8. Clothing Store/Kitchen
9. Stable
10. Stores
11. SS Orderly Room
12. SS Quarters
13. Ablutions
14. SS Canteen/WC
15. Garage/Workshops
16. Guardroom

The numbers of workers on Alderney varied, however, Major Pantcheff does attempt to give a average figure for a mid-term point – May 1943 – when there was a total of about 4,000 workers of which 2,200 were OT workers only and broke down as follows: 700 Russians, 400 volunteers of mixed European nationalities, 100 women, mostly French, 300 French Jews and 700 German.

Sylt Camp

Of all the camps on Alderney, the real 'lowest of the low' was the Sylt camp where the poor unfortunate 1,000 workers which formed the SS *Baubrigade* I (SS Construction Brigade No 1) were located. The SS staff who acted as guards and administrators came from a concentration camp at Neuengamme near Hamburg, whilst the 'workforce' were inmates from a camp at Sachenausen near Berlin. Half were Russian POWs or partisans, 200 Germans (conscientious objectors, criminals, political prisoners and 'workshy', etc), whilst the rest were European political prisoners. They had arrived by sea in two batches on 3 and 5 March 1943 – in battened-down holds without water or sanitation, despite the ship's captain's protests. Last to disembark were six bloodhounds. Sylt Camp had its security raised to a higher level than the other three camps, with a heavily wired inner compound for the prisoners and an outer compound for the guards and administrative staff. There were concrete sentry posts at strategic locations (see map on page 113).

> *'Every day the Camp Commandant made a habit of beating any man he found not standing properly to attention or who had not made his bed properly or did not execute a drill movement properly. The beatings were carried out on the head, face or body, with a stick about 2.5cm in diameter. The Camp Commandant's assistant also beat workers daily with a stick of the same thickness on all parts of the body until their faces were covered with blood and they could not rise from the ground, when he would call on the prisoners mates to carry the prostrate body away.'*

That was the type of treatment which the survivors told 'Bunny' Pantcheff about – and there was worse, when some were beaten to death. Not only did the OT staff and the SS beat the workers, but they also stole their meagre rations and sold them, so that

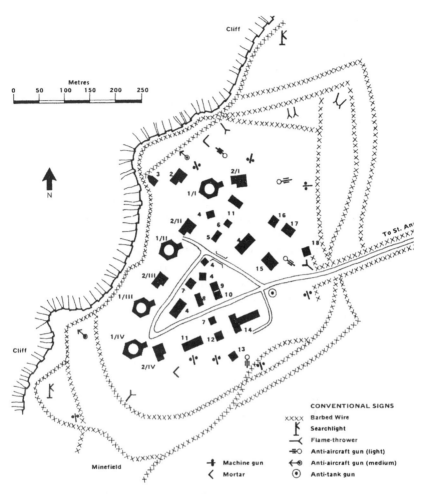

⊙ WEST BATTERIE

CONVENTIONAL SIGNS

xxxx Barbed Wire
Ϟ Searchlight
⊢ Flame-thrower
⊷ Anti-aircraft gun (light)
⟵ Anti-aircraft gun (medium)
⊙ Anti-tank gun
⊣ Machine gun
< Mortar

1. 15 cm gun site
2. Crew bunker
3. Fire control
4. Ammunition magazine
5. Armourer
6. Orderly Room
7. Water tank
8. Quartermaster
9. Clerks
10. Tool shop
11. Store hut
12. Ablutions
13. Soak-away
14. Canteen
15. Generator
16. M.I. Room
17. Junior Officers/Senior NCOs
18. Garage

the workers were soon seriously undernourished as one explained to Major Pantcheff:

'Within a month of my arrival at Norderney the average death rate was two to three per day. At the time of our arrival we had been in normal health, but constant beatings and starvation diet had reduced us to an extremely feeble condition.'

The camp was run by SS *Haupsturmfuehrer* Maximillian List, an experienced hand from Neuengamme, who had a chalet built just outside the perimeter, with an underground passage leading to the heating/bath house so that he could come and go as he pleased. His deputies – SS *Obersturmfuehrer* Klebeck and Braun, were both experienced murderers like their commandant. Braun (a certifed uncured syphilitic) took over when List left in the spring of 1944, posted to Oslo. Being SS his immediate superior was in Germany, so he did not have to obey the local commander and was his own master. So he did virtually as he pleased, withholding the prisoners rations and Red Cross parcels and selling them in France. The camp was run on the 'trusty' system, the 'kapos' being chosen from among the German prisoners, and they were inclined to be even more brutal than the SS guards, receiving privileges for maintaining harsh discipline. When they eventually left in June 1944[1], they took with them all the surviving prisoners, who were then sent to other camps, including Buchenwald. Sylt Camp remained unused and was allowed to drop to pieces, much of it being burnt as firewood which was always in short supply in the other camps.

Notes

1. They had left in mid-December 1943, following a strong protest from the commander of LXXIV Army Corps (*Generaloberst* Erich Marcks), but returned in February 1944. Their final departure was deliberately timed so that they could be 'hidden away' from the Allies .

CHAPTER SEVEN

1944 – D DAY AND THE HUNGER WINTER

Fortress Status

On 3 March 1944, the Channel Islands were given fortress status being classified as *Festungen* to join eleven other fortresses (declared on 19 January 1944) along the Atlantic Wall. The original eleven were: Ijmuiden and the Hook of Holland in the Netherlands; Dunkirk, Boulogne and Le Havre in the Fifteenth Army sector along the Channel; Cherbourg, St Malo, Brest, Lorient and St Nazaire in the Seventh Army zone; and the Gironde River estuary which led to Bordeaux. At the same time as adding the Channel Islands they also took in two more coastal fortresses, namely the harbours at Calais and La Pallice-La Rochelle, although they had already been given considerable attention earlier.*[1] Whilst in general terms, there was more building activity along the Channel and Atlantic coasts – the OT constructing in six months, almost half as many again concrete structures (8,478 to be exact) as they had built in the whole of the previous two and a half years, activity in the Channel Islands decreased, the labour force on all the islands gradually dropping from an all-time high of 7,500 in November 1943 to

Although there was a steady drain of OT labour leaving the islands, there was still a fair amount left, such as this assorted 'gang' of French labourers. Société Jersiaise

some 3,890 in May 1944. In his Archive Book on the OT, Michael Ginns shows the rundown quoted in the *Festpistab* Building Progress Reports as follows:

November 1943 – 7,500; December; 1943 – 6,700; January 1944 – 4,200; February 1944 – 4,500; March 1944 – 3,900; April 1944 – 3,900; May 1944 – 3,890

He also quotes from one civilian observer that the OT staff had been selling off – at very low prices – loads of wood, bags of cement, etc: '... the Todts are making a little money before they leave!'

Probably the most evil of the civil labour overseers were, as mentioned in the last chapter, the SS *Baubrigade* 1 (1st SS Construction Brigade) , who ran the Sylt concentration camp on Alderney, where some 1,000 inmates, half of which were Russian POWs, were subjected to daily torture and brutality. They had arrived as explained, from another concentration camp near Berlin in March 1943 and those who remained alive were shipped back to the mainland in June 1944, destined for other camps including Buchenwald. Other OT workers were more fortunate, Gilbert van Grieken, for example, a young Dutchman, who had been forcibly conscripted as an OT worker, was lucky enough to be changed from OT work to working for the military in the harbour at St Peter Port. This also saved him being sent back to the mainland in 'slave-ship' conditions, with

Some foreign slave/OT labourers were still on the islands when the Germans surrendered, like these Spaniards, finally waving goodbye before starting their journey home - but what reception will they get from Franco? Société Jersiaise

the added risk of being bombed en route, like the *Minotaur* which was sunk on 7 July 1944, with the loss of 250 lives, including many forced labourers.

Despite this rundown of building labour, which meant a slowdown in completing all the planned defences indeed some were never finished; Hitler still insisted that the Islands must be defended to '... the last man and the last bullet' and he personally approved the appointment of the three fortress commanders – *Generallieutant* von Schmettow to Guernsey, *Oberst* Heine to Jersey and Maj Schwalm to Alderney. They would also have to defend their *festungen* with the manpower already on the Islands as no more could be spared from the mainland. It would still remain the responsibility of OB West (von Rundstedt) to maintain supplies of food, ammunition, equipment and fuel, to keep them functioning. This was easy enough for the Fuehrer to order, but probably neither he nor anybody else realised at that stage the true impact of the enforced isolation of the Islands that would soon follow on from the Allied invasion of France

Nevertheless, as this extract from a speech given by von Schmettow to soldiers in Jersey shows, the German garrison (or at least their top brass) were determined to hang on, viz:

'The German soldier, with building pioneers, supported by the OT men, have made this Island impregnable. As a result of hard work and iron execution to duty, the Atlantic wall is the best defence work in history, which is what our Fuehrer ordered. The German soldier, true to his flag, will hold the position to which the Fuehrer has appointed him, until the last drop of blood. We, the Occupation Forces in Jersey, are today conscious of the warriors of Stalingrad and trusting in our power and strength, in our faith in our Fuehrer, and, pledging increasing devotion to duty and preparedness, we also will hold the Island in the coming fourth year. When the hour of trial comes it will find us ready. Heil Hitler!'

The runup to 'D-Day' *The Sixth of June conference.*

All OB West's corps and divisional commanders were ordered to attend a conference to be held at Rennes on 6 June. The aim was clearly to discuss strategy. However, Von Rundstedt could not have chosen a more ill-timed day to hold his conference, which shows that the Germans did not know the exact date of the coming invasion. Von Schmettow had left Guernsey on 4 June, bound for St Malo and from there travelled to Rennes via Granville. There was a preliminary conference before the main one, at which Gen Erich Marcks, the capable and well-liked commander of LXXXIV Corps, which would bear the brunt of the Allied invasion, said that he expected the Allies to invade by the middle of June at the very latest. There was much speculation as to where the Allies would strike, the Pas de Calais area still being the odds-on favourite, although Hitler also considered Normandy to be very likely. After the preliminary conference von Schmettow inspected the Atlantic Wall fortifications, which also included many radar stations and V weapon sites in the Cotentin peninsula, as well as significant coastal defences in such areas as *Festung Cherbourg*. Privately, he did not consider that the defences were as good as his on the Channel Islands. He was at Granville when the invasion news came and he immediately made contact with the Islands. However, all was reported as being: 'under control' and there had been no attempt to invade, but naturally he had wanted to get back as quickly as possible. Despite almost continual air-raids he managed to catch a boat and reached Guernsey early on the morning of the 7th. As Charles Cruickshank says in his excellent book on the occupation:

'*From this moment the Islands became progressively more isolated. Many vessels which had served them were lost in the invasion battles, and the few that were left had little fuel. Rhine barges were chosen to supply the Islands because their low build made them difficult radar targets, but they could only be used in calm weather. When it was rough, the* Robert Mueller, *which had carried the deportees in 1942, was called in.*'[2]

To the Islanders and the Garrision, the most obvious aspect of Allied activity in the Spring and early Summer of 1944 was a marked increase in air activity. The islands fortifications were bombed, port facilities attacked, also shipping – some twenty-five ships operating in Channel Islands waters being sunk or damaged. Undoubtedly part of this was deliberately done to isolate the islands from the mainland and to give the impression that they might be used as 'stepping stones' for an assault upon the mainland of Europe, however, much of the increased activity was just a part of the overall bigger picture that was leading up to the launching of the Second Front.

One Jersey woman who kept a diary throughout the Occupation, started her 1st January 1944 entry as follows:

'We enter this year fully believing that we shall be liberated before its close, hoping even, that during its first half, we shall be freed, not only our island, but Europe. But, what bloodshed, what terrible things must happen before the enemy gives in.'

Five months later, her 6 June entry began:

'... What a day! At last the invasion of France so long talked about has taken place! We can hardly take it in yet. So far, everything is quiet and as usual here, except that one has seen very few Germans about today... They are all at their guns and under the ground in their fortifications.'[3]

Oberst (later Generalmajor) Siegfried Heine, who was Festungskommandant for Jersey in 1944, then commander of German troops on Guernsey. Holder of the Ritterkreuz with Swords which he had won in the Great War. Jens Ulrich Heine

She goes on to explain how all night long on 5 June, there had been the noise of aircraft passing continually and of constant anti-aircraft fire as the Germans responded. That evening, there was a proclamation published in the newspaper which read:

To the population of the Island of Jersey:

Germany's enemy is on the point of attacking French soil. I expect the population of Jersey to keep its head and to remain calm, and to refrain from acts of sabotage and from hostile acts against the German forces, even should the fighting spread to Jersey. At the first signs of unrest or trouble I will close the streets to all traffic and will secure hostages. Attacks against the German forces will be punished by death.

Signed: Heine, Oberst Der Kommandant der Festung Jersey.

From then on all German forces continually wore their combat equipment (ie: steel helmet, basic personal equipment, small arms, etc) and were on duty at their various battle stations day and night. All beaches were closed to the public, whilst public entertainment – such as cinema shows, sports games, or public gatherings – was not permitted. Bus services were curtailed and telephone exchanges taken over for exclusive military use. On 10 July, following the Allied capture of

Cherbourg three days earlier, expectations that the Channel Islands would be attacked seemed so likely, that a week's emergency ration of foodstuffs were issued to the public and first aid posts were set up at various locations to deal with expected civilian casualties. Nothing of course happened.

The Dame of Sark learns of 'D-Day'

Another woman on another island had also had her sleep disturbed by the Allied bombers overhead on the night of 5/6 June, but she was told personally of the invasion by Sark's German doctor who came into her study very mysteriously the following morning, closed the door tightly and said in a low whisper:

'"You must tell nobody or I will be shot, but I have news for you. The Allies have landed on the French coast between Cherbourg and Le Havre." He added hurriedly, "Of course it is probably only another raid like the one at Dieppe, but I will come back when I can tell you what is happening."[4]

He disappeared before she could say anything, so she immediately rushed to her own hidden radio and listened to the BBC, which confirmed what he had said. Thereafter, she listened regularly and had to avoid showing the '... slightest signs of excitement.'

From then on everyone on the Islands could clearly hear the thunder of guns in the day, accompanied at night by flashes and lights as the Allies advanced along the coast of France, just a few miles away from them over the water – how frustrating it must have been in one way, but no doubt they were pleased not to be on the receiving end of all the shot and shell.

Use of the underground hospitals

In addition to the increased Allied sea and air activity, together with the far off sights and sounds of warfare on the mainland, the islanders also began to notice the arrival of German casualties for treatment in the underground hospitals on Jersey and Guernsey. These were enormous underground structures which had been hollowed out on both islands and still remain today (see Chapter 9 for details of how they can now be visited). In the summer of 1944, however, they had a more practical use. The Guernsey hospital, for example, was built at La Vassalerie Road, St Andrew's, in the middle of the island.

From the outside it looks nondescript, just an inconspiciuous tunnel entrance, which is what the Germans intended, however, beyond the entrance lies a complex of operating theatres, wards, staff sleeping quarters, kitchens, a dispensary, laboratory, vast storage areas and even a cinema. Work had begun on the complex in the winter of 1941, three years later it was still not entirely finished. The work had been undertaken by hundreds of foreign workers under the supervision of the OT, compelled to work like slaves. The entire structure was air-conditioned, centrally-heated and had water and electricty laid on.

The hospital in Jersey at St Lawrence was equally large, the tunnels blasted out of the shale using explosives, then hand-excavated with picks and shovels by the forced labourers, who worked like 'ants' in the complex of kilometre-long tunnels. One estimate said that some 13,600 tons of shale, rock and earth were removed. It had in fact been originally intended as a bomb-proof artillery barracks and ammunition store, but was later converted into a hospital, some 4,000 tonnes of concrete being used to clad the walls. The 900 plus medical corps servicemen on the islands, including female nursing staff, used these facilities to treat hundreds of casualties, shipped over from St Malo during July 1944.

Naval activity – *Batterie Bluecher is shelled*

Increased Allied naval activity continued after D-Day and this sometimes led to engagements with shore-based batteries, especially when they were interfering with Allied movement on the mainland. For example in June 1944, the four 15cm guns of *Batterie Bluecher* had sufficient range to be able to engage American troops in the Cotentin peninsula and did so, causing casualties. It was decided that, instead of bombing them – due to the considerable anti-aircraft protection on Alderney – a surface ship would be used to deal with them. British battleship HMS *Rodney* which had been helping to support the landings was asked to do the honours and on 12 August, from the area near Cherbourg she bombarded the shore batteries at a range of some 25 miles, using a spotter aircraft. Seventy-two of her massive 16 inch shells were fired and they damaged three of the guns of *Batterie Bluecher* killing two and injuring several others amongst the gun crews. Nevertheless, the damaged guns were repaired and back in action by November.

Another naval engagement took place 13/14 August, to the south of Guernsey, where HMS *Saumerez* and *Onslaught* were on patrol. Part of their duties were to send a signal to the German Military Governor of the islands to surrender immediately, however, as expected their signal received no reply. The two destroyers were mainly there to prevent enemy shipping movements between the islands and were shortly joined by motor torpedo (PT) boats of the United States 34th Squadron, operating under the control of their HQ ship USS *Borum*. That evening at about 2200 hrs, four 'M' Class minesweepers of the *Kriegsmarine* 24th Minesweeper Flotilla, two harbour security boats and the coaster MV *Spinel* left St Helier in convoy, bound for St Peter Port. Radar contact was made with the convoy at about 2300 hrs and two PT boats went to investigate. However, the German convoy had also spotted the Allied ships on their radar and swiftly requested support from two costal artillery batteries on Jersey which began shelling the American vessels. The German ships then joined in and at about three quarters of a mile range, the two PT boats launched torpedoes at the nearest minesweeper. Neither torpedo hit, nor did the heavy shelling do any damage to either US PT boat which then broke off the engagement.

At 0010 hours one of the British destroyers sighted the German convoy at a range of some 6000 yards and took up a parallel course. Starshells were fired by both sides and a fierce battle ensued, which also involved the shore batteries as the British destroyers chased the enemy convoy into port. A considerable amount of ammuntion was fired by both sides and there were hits confirmed on the ships of both navies. As a result casualties were considerable, the Germans suffering twelve killed and twenty-one wounded, whilst five of the HMS *Saumerez* officers were wounded (four seriously) and HMS *Onslaught* had seven wounded. Reporting on the action, the commander of HMS *Saumerez* wrote:

> *'It was disappointing that more positive results had not been obtained. It was considered that the enemy handled their ships with ability and determination and the large volume of tracer fire they produced made spotting difficult. Also their use of smoke was very effective and in the confined waters had a larger influence on the course of events than it would have done in open waters.'*[5]

The Allied efforts to stop inter-island shipping seems to have waned after August 1944. This was probably due to the capture of the supply ports on the adjacent French coast, which meant there was much less traffic going to the islands.

On towards the 'Hunger Winter'

'11.8.44... Yesterday St Malo fell. We are finally cut off. The day was extremely clear and we could distinctly see the clouds of smoke rising above the shattered city out there across the sea. ... Our situation is extraordinary; we and the Jersey people are alike prisoners of the islands... As the map shows, these small islands now lie in insignificant isolation at the centre of a British-dominated area. The dogs of war have passed us by. We joke about the forgetfulness of the British at leaving us behind.' [6]

Baron von Aufsess, head of Civil Affairs at the Feldkommandantur. His wartime diary was first published in English in 1985.
IWM-HU 25912

So wrote the urbane Baron von Aufsess, Head of Civil Affairs in the *Feldkommandantur*, in his diary. The situation did get progressively more difficult for everyone, as various methods of resupply were tried and failed. Initially the Luftwaffe's faithful old standby *Tante Ju* was used to bring in stores, but flights soon became less and less frequent, then stopped altogether. Another suggestion was made to use submarines, especially as it was also decided to use St Peter Port on Guernsey as an operational U-boat base. Clearly suitable cargoes would need to be 'luxury' items as the payload was small (twenty-five tons approximately per U-Boat) – such as fats, soap, razor blades, or sugar. However, this idea also came to naught.

It soon dawned upon the German High Command that the Allies did not intend to invade the islands at all, but rather to leave them alone until they were forced through hunger into submission. It was too late now to do as Rommel had demanded months before, and remove the garrison to fight in France, whilst the redundant OT workers and SS penal brigade – which had to be 'hidden' from the

Allies at all costs – had all gone. The drastic alternative that was now considered was not only to evacuate the entire civilian population, but to ask the British to do so, or, as an alternative at least to send the people food supplies. During September the message was passed to the British that food supplies for the civilan population were all but exhausted and that the Germans were willing to allow either for food to be sent in, or for the evacuation to the UK of all but men who were fit enough to fight. If these proposals were agreed then action to put them into effect was to be taken immediately.

The proposals received a mixed reaction in London – the Chiefs of Staff had no objections as they no longer saw the islands as a military threat, but preferred the resupply option as it would require far less shipping. The Home Office also supported this option as they were convinced that many islanders would refuse to leave and it would be bad propaganda to forcibly uproot the civil population after they had withstood the long years of occupation. Something clearly had to be done or the Germans might be able to win a major propaganda coup by claiming that the Allies were leaving the poor islanders to starve. Prime Minister Winston Churchill, however, had very firm views. He had fully endorsed the isolation of the islands from the mainland and agreed the proposal that the garrison should be starved out – '... Let 'em starve. No fighting. They can rot at their leisure' – that is what he put in a marginal note on the proposed plan, but nevertheless he did perfectly understand the civilian implications of such a policy. Charles Cruickshank quotes from a Churchill minute dated 27 September which said:

'I am entirely opposed to our sending any rations to the Channel Islands ostensibly for the civil population but in fact enabling the German garrison to prolong their resistance. I therefore prefer to evacuate the women and children at once, and I would offer that men capable of bearing arms should be bound not to take any further part in the war. It is possible that the Germans would accept this, as with the reduction of the population their existing food supplies would last them longer. I would rather face this than go on feeding them. It is no part of our job to feed armed Germans and enable them to prolong their hold on British territory.'

The impasse was eventually broken, when it was mutually

The arrival of the Swedish ship SS Vega chartered by the International Red Cross to bring food to the starving islanders did much to alleviate the suffering of the civilians. IWM-HU25968

agreed that the International Red Cross would be allowed to send a ship – the SS *Vega* – loaded with over 100,000 food parcels plus other items (such as invalid diet parcels, medical supplies, soap, salt and even cigarettes), to the beleaguered islanders. The ship arrived just after Christmas and discharged its cargo on the 27th. Whilst the garrision was strictly prohibited from partaking of anything sent in, the arrival of these much needed items did – in German eyes – put the onus for looking after the civilian population firmly onto the International Red Cross, which lightened the load on the garrison. 'The Red Cross ship has arrived!' wrote Nan le Ruez excitedly in her diary, 'one can hardly believe it after all the disappointments.'

However, whilst the civilian population had been: 'saved from starvation', the rationing for both them and for the garrison remained severely limited. Thus began what the Germans called: *Die grosse Hungerzeit*. Here is how one member of MG Battalion 16 described his feelings during the 'Great Hunger':

> '*At the end of August our rations were reduced for the first time, and, at the end of September, a second time. This*

Red Cross parcels were distributed to the islanders, such as here at Les Riches, St Peter Port, Guernsey. IWM-HU 25920

On board the SS Vega a German officer talks with Red Cross representatives. The garrison did not receive any of the food parcels.
Société Jersiaise

particularly affected the bread ration and the soup from the Company kitchen became noticeably thinner and less nourishing. It was in October when we first felt really hungry. We needed additional food, jam was running short – jam and artificial honey being the basis of breakfast in the German Army. We were sent into the hills to harvest the abundant quantity of blackberries, but they only lasted for a short time and we ended up with sugar instead. In November rations were cut again and the pangs of hunger worsened. The bread got worse as substitutes were mixed with the flour. We began to eat stinging nettles and grew to like them. Inspite of orders to the contrary, everybody tried to find something edible in his vicinity. There was hardly any farmland in our area. The farms were small and the farmers could not give us much, although they were always ready to barter (by the end of the war most of us had lost our watches). Potatoes in the soup were replaced by turnips. Finally, we got potatoes only on a Sunday, otherwise only turnips, turnips, turnips!'

After Christmas, the rations were again reduced and this happened practically every month as the last 'terrible months' of the siege began. The reduced diet had its effect upon the efficiency of the garrison and daily duties had to be curtailed as he remembers,

'Drill and exercising disappeared almost completely. Before we had got up at 6am, now it was 7am and 8am on Sundays. Midday rest had been 12.30 to 1.30, now it was 12.30 to 2.30 – that was an order! By day we received a lot of instruction and theoretical training. In the evening our small rations were distributed (there was seldom any quarreling) and gulped down ravenously. We then went straight to bed. You lay on your side, knees pulled up to the chin to try to subdue the hungry feeling.'

Even the German system of ration distribution worked against the hungry men. The laid down procedure was for two deliveries of food daily – one at noon, the other in the evening. Soldiers were expected to keep some of the evening delivery for breakfast the next day, as all that was served in the morning was ersatz coffee. This worked perfectly well normally, but in the *Grosse Hungerzeit* everything was wolfed down in the evening, so nothing remained for the morning.

> *'An order was then issued that we had to cut a slice of bread from our evening ration, put it into an envelope and hand it over to the corporal for storage until the next morning! The second part of the order said that each morsel of the ration had to be chewed 30-32 times to make maximum use of it. In future we were to eat together and the corporal had to ensure that every man chewed properly!'*

One can imagine how this order was received by the soldiers. They had to obey the part about cutting off the slice of bread, but everyone kept their own envelopes and cut off small pieces during the evening when the pangs of hunger became unbearable, so:

> *'... by the morning a piece the size of a postage stamp was all that remained.'*

This may all sound bizarre behaviour but it was no different to that of most of the civilian population. Guernseyman Raymond Falla commented in a tape he made for the Imperial War Museum about the subject of dividing up rations:

> *'It was a sight to see four grown up men grumbling over a slice of bread, in that we weighed our bread on letter scales to make sure that no-one had more than his fair share, because one was tempted sometimes to cut a bigger slice off the loaf, so we weighed every slice of bread and sometimes quarrelled over it. People got very bad and it was a relief to us all that the* Vega *came along on six occasions and provided us with sustenance which virtually saved the lives of many who did not have the privilege to have any land at their disposal, or relatives with land. It was a tough time.'*[7]

First civilian casualties. As one might expect some members of the Nazi garrison were not

The Hunger Winter. A rabbit like this one would make a welcome addition to the spartan rations which the garrison had to exist on during Die Grosse Hungerzeit – the time of great hunger during the winter of 1944/45.
Hans-Gerhard Sandmann

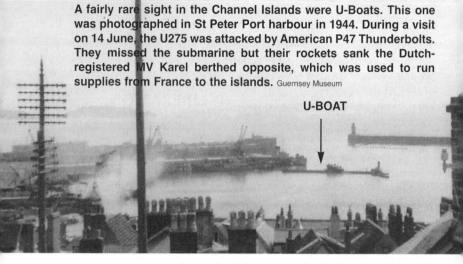

A fairly rare sight in the Channel Islands were U-Boats. This one was photographed in St Peter Port harbour in 1944. During a visit on 14 June, the U275 was attacked by American P47 Thunderbolts. They missed the submarine but their rockets sank the Dutch-registered MV Karel berthed opposite, which was used to run supplies from France to the islands. Guernsey Museum

U-BOAT

averse to using physical violence to obtain food and on 25 August the first civilian casualties occurred, caused by members of the German garrison trying to steal food, when Mr Jehan of St Saviour's was killed and his son wounded, whilst they were trying to drive off German marauders. To be fair to the military this was immediately stamped on by the authorities, who imposed the death penalty for the violation of food regulations, on 1 September.

Meanwhile at the top

As though Gen von Schmettow hadn't got enough on his plate, he now found himself in a power struggle with ruthless Nazi *Vizeadmiral* Friedrich Hueffmeier, who had taken over as SEEKO-KI, then became von Schmettow's Chief of Staff in September 1944, von Aufsess commenting in his diary:

> *'In Guernsey Admiral Hueffmeier has succeeded in getting himself appointed Chief of Staff. The General will now be more than ever pushed into the background; he is no match for such a ruthless ambitious man.'*

Von Aufsess's comments would come true just a few months later.

Notes

1. See Chapter 6 of *The Atlantic Wall* by Professor Alan Wilt.
2. *The German Occupation of the Channel Islands* by Charles Cruickshank.
3. *Jersey Occupation Diary* by Nan Le Ruez.
4. *Dame of Sark* by Sibyl Hathaway.
5. *CIOS Review* 1982 – quoted in an article on the battle by D Kreckler
6. *The von Aufsess Occupation Diary*.
7. IWM Dept of Sound Records Accession No 01000/4.

CHAPTER EIGHT

1945 – SURRENDER AND LIBERATION

The hunger continues

While the continued generous assistance of the Red Cross via the good ship Vega certainly eased the hunger problems on the islands, they did not solve them completely and both captors and captives alike suffered accordingly. Occasionally there were unexpected 'windfalls' of food – likened by some to 'Biblical Miracles', such as the time when the beach at St Ouen, Jersey, was suddenly covered with small octopuses, which must have been swept up from the Mediterranean by the Gulf Stream, then stunned suddenly by meeting the colder water and washed ashore. The health authorities issued an edict that they shouldn't be eaten until they had been properly tested, but no-one – neither soldier nor civilian alike took any notice. As one German soldier recalled:

> 'For days there was only slaughtering, cooking and eating. I have always had an aversion to reptiles and even touching a worm is a great effort, but being so hungry I dealt with the

It was on beaches like this one that the unexpected glut of small octopuses arrived. Such beaches were not as safe as they might at first appear, being heavily mined and covered in obstacles which were also often fitted with explosive charges. IWM - HU 29131

octopuses like a butcher. ... There was a real public festival on the beach. Soldiers and civilians mingled and for a few days the prohibited area signs were disregarded. Hunger had taken possession of everybody without heeding nationality and we felt we were all in the same boat.'

The glut of these strange sea creatures lasted for about three weeks, then everything returned to normal and all that remained were the usual slim pickings of limpets off the rocks, the rocky coasts and severe currents making fishing from the shoreline almost impossible everywhere.

My redoubtable relative, Colonel Heber Forty commented that the entire occupation was 'five years of hell for the Guernsey people', during which time they were reduced to walking scarecrows and some nearly starved to death. He spent many of his days foraging for food. He was fortunate to have a garden which helped a lot and a bicycle which enabled him to get to the beaches and look for shellfish (he wangled a special permit to go onto them despite the beaches being mined). He says:

'I managed to get some shellfish. I also ate snails, boiled with cabbage, got blood from the slaughterhouse and baked in the oven big pies of blood, vegetables and flour, if available, or any kind of bean of which I grew many. In this way I managed to stay alive, though I lost weight.'

He was also worried by the stories of hungry German soldiers breaking into civilian homes, so he barricaded his house and garden with barbed wire and slept in a lower room with his loaded shotgun by his side.

A change of commander

'1.3.45. Yesterday brought shattering news. At lunchtime Heider informed me that the General and Helldorf had been dismissed from office. From 12 hours, midday, today Hueffmeier takes over as Commander-in-Chief of the Channel Islands. Other far reaching changes in command have also been ordered. The whole thing smacks of a putsch or coup e'etat. What lies behind it all is as yet no means clear, but I suspect it is a move long since carefully planned.'

So wrote Baron von Aufsess in his diary and his suspicions were correct. For many months the rabid Nazi *VizeAdmiral* Friedrich Hueffmeier had been plotting to oust General von

A change of commander. Vizeadmiral Friedrich Hueffmeier and Generalmajor Rudolf Wulf, the two victors in the March 1945 coup d'etat, are seen here some months later after the German surrender, when they arrived in Plymouth on 12 May, before proceeding to London for interrogation. IWM - MH 3901

Schmettow and succeeded at the end of February 1945, von Schmettow announcing that he was giving up command of 319 ID and retiring to Germany for 'health reasons' where he would be transferred to the reserve. *Oberst* (later *Generalmajor*) Siegfried Heine would become the temporary commander of the division but would later be replaced by *Generalmajor* Rudolf Wulf, (von Aufsess described Wulf as being the achetypal professional soldier, with no personal warmth or affability and no interest in anything but purely military affairs). Hueffmeier would become *Befehlshaber*, the post for which he had schemed. There was also a 'naval takeover' of the other senior posts, with *Kaptain sur Zee* Kleve taking over command in Jersey and *Kapitan sur Zee* Reich in Guernsey. Hueffmeier 'nailed his colours to the mast' in a speech he made in the Odeon Cinema soon after he had assumed command, in which he said: 'I have only one aim and that is to hold out until final victory.' And so obsessed was he with this aim he is said to have stated more than once that he would make his men eat grass before he

133

allowed them to surrender. More indicative of the true feelings of those on the island was an attempt made on 18 March to kill Wulf, whilst he was travelling by car in Jersey. A bomb was thrown at the car, but it bounced off one of the wheels and failed to explode. It is unclear whether this, or other violent incidents which took place during March 1945, were civilian acts of violence or came from within disaffected elements of the military. For example, on 7 March, the Palace Hotel, St Helier, was blown up killing nine Germans and injuring others, the official account said that a fire had broken out and the Germans, who didn't trust the local fire brigade, had put explosive charges around the fire, which had then blown up. However, another version – and probably nearer the truth – was that there had been an explosion (sabotage presumably), which had killed a much larger number of Germans and it had started the fire, which had burnt down the hotel. Undoubtedly there were some Marxists within the Wehrmacht forces on the islands and in the civilian population, and their activities were becoming more vocal. 'Soldiers of Jersey,' read one of their leaflets, 'how long do you intend to take part in this, the biggest deception of all time? How long do you want to stay here and starve?' It went on to advocate that, when 'the signal' was given, all officers should be arrested or shot, whilst saboteurs were to be allowed to go free. 'Free yourselves through a great act of liberation' it concluded.

Certainly one civilian, Mr Norman Le Brocq, who was a member of the Jersey Communist Party, was convinced that the blowing up of the Palace Hotel was the work of disaffected German servicemen and not civilians. In a recording he made for the Imperial War Museum (Accession No 0010101/2) he explains that he knew an 'anti-Nazi German', called Muelbach, who told him:

'...they (ie: the German senior staff) were planning a commando raid on the French coast there (ie: in the Palace Hotel). They'd held quite a successful commando raid on Granville ...Now they were planning another one. Apparently the soldiers' committee got to know that this high level, high brass conference was due to take place at the Palace. They blew the Palace Hotel up with quite a number of officers, naval officer, casualties. The place was quite literally razed to the ground and the explosion was – I was working the town that morning and there was a fantastic bumpf. My next door neighbour was*

Muelbach. He told me just what I have just said, that, "Yes, we heard that they were planning another commando raid, we decided to stop it and we were able to assemble sufficient explosives in the cellar to set it off."... That was the most significant action I think.'

Raids on France

The raids which Mr Le Brocq mentions were indeed planned and executed against the French coast during March/April 1945. The first was a naval-led raid, when on 8 March, thirteen ships – four E-Boats, three *artillerietraeger* and six other vessels, set out to raid the small port of Granville which the Americans were using as a supply base. The force, under an ex-U Boat commander *Kapitanleutnant* Mohr, managed to get ashore, blow up several ships and severely damage the port installations and lock gates. Then they brought heavy fire to bear on the local military barracks – occupied by American troops – and freed a number of German prisoners. They returned in triumph, bringing back an empty collier and enroute, severely damaging an American patrol boat which had to be beached near Cancale. Total losses were small – just one minesweeper, which ran aground at Granville in the low tide, could not be refloated and had to be sunk.

Then it was the Army's turn to show their mettle, with a commando-type raid on the Cotentin peninsula in early April. Target for the raid was to be an important railway bridge just south of Cherbourg, which, if destroyed, would seriously affect

Raids on France. Close-up of an artillerietraeger gives a good idea of its firepower. Three of these vessels provided much of the 'muscle' for the highly successful raid on Granville, 8 March 1945.
Société Jersiaise

the American supply lines. The raiding party of twenty-one men, under a *Leutenant* Maltzahn, adjutant of the Guernsey-based infantry regiment, comprised: two NCOs, 17 engineers and two naval signallers, one of whom operated the radio whilst the other carried the batteries. The operator was *Funkobergefreiter* Bernd Westoff, one of the most efficient operators in the islands' naval signals. In a postwar article (published in the *CIOS Review* of 1986), he gave a graphic account of the raid, beginning with the hard physical training they had undertaken for some four weeks prior to the operation. Despite the food shortages all taking part had been allowed extra rations. He had to wear army uniform and maintain communications back to Guernsey. On 4 April, the raiders had embarked on a minesweeper, sailed first to Sark in order to conceal their true destination, then on to the proper landing site in France. They landed without being spotted, using two rubber boats, but then took no precautions to hide the boats or return them to the minesweeper. During the landing one of the party fell overboard and had to be rescued, in the process losing all his personal arms, ammunition, rations and explosives (each man carried 16kg of explosives). They then set off towards their objective, crossing an old German minefield and passing close to American billets, where they heard the GIs singing and joking loudly. They then hid in undergrowth near a busy road, waiting for last light and watching a seemingly endless stream of US vehicles passing by.

At dusk, Westoff sent a short signal to say all was well and his transmission was swiftly acknowledged. Then, everything started to go wrong. On inspecting the bridge, it was decided that the explosives they had brought were insufficient to demolish it, so Maltzahn decided to attack Cherbourg railway station instead. They marched along towards the port quite openly, answering in French when challenged and, just before they reached the station, the two sailors hid near the roadside at an agreed rendezvous and the rest moved on. Almost immediately they were spotted, illuminated by powerful searchlights and came under heavy small-arms fire. The two sailors waited anxiously, but only *Leutnant* Maltzahn returned alone. After some while the three men decided to make for the coast, but were soon intercepted and engaged by members of the French Maquis (the local resistance fighters), the sailors becoming separated from their commander in the confusion which followed. Leaderless, the two sailors continued to make their way towards the beach and then hid in the loft of an old deserted barn. Westhoff enciphered a signal saying that the raid had failed and that the raiders had been dispersed. Then, with Guernsey's agreement, he destroyed the radio and burnt all the codes and other confidential documents. 'At dawn,' recounted Westhoff,

> 'four jeeps mounting heavy machine guns approached the barn. We were told to come out and surrender and shots were fired into the roof. We climbed down the ladder from the loft to surrender.'

He says that both sides were scared stiff of each other and that at one stage both they and the GIs faced each other all with their hands up. Then they were ordered to sit on the bonnet of one of the jeeps and driven through Cherbourg with the local population shouting and spitting at them. Westhoff and his companion would be interrogated, give no information away apart from their name and number and then sent to a POW camp.

The only member of the raiding party to reach Guernsey safely – though wounded – was the raid commander, *Leutnant* Malzhan and his report on what they had seen led to the 15cm guns of *Batterie Bluecher* on Alderney, successfully engaging the American supply dumps, ammunition depots and tank/vehicle parks in the Cherbourg area. The final twist in the story was the fact that, unbeknown to Westhoff, the radio codewords had been changed back in Guernsey and, instead of his all important message opening with the codeword: 'raid failed', the opening codeword had been translated as: 'raid successful'. Fortunately, the rest of his transmission was decoded before an entirely wrong message was sent on to the German higher authorities!

Moves towards surrender

The 'Hunger Winter' eventually gave way to spring, von Aufsess remarking in his diary towards the end of April that:

> '... if wars could be won by flowers, we could from these islands conquer the whole continent. Never has there been a spring with such a lot of blossom.'

Nan le Ruez also mentions the change in the weather, but is more concerned with the possibilities that spring will bring release from their long captivity. She also talks about cases of disaffection within the German garrison, how soldiers have told her neighbours that, once the British land they will shoot their officers and put up their hands. '... Many talk like that now.' Heavy bombing and explosions could now be heard from mainland France as the Allied troops dealt with those 'fortresses' which had been holding out. In fact one of them – Dunkirk – would hold out until 10 May 1945, being the last French town to be liberated. 'Mr Le Brun' she comments,

> *'says that the Germans would surrender here if they were offered a good dinner! They are starving. Two have been shot dead for stealing potatoes in a field at St John's.'*

For their part the British were still uncertain as to whether the Germans would fight or not. Although they knew that the garrison had been – and still was – suffering from malnutrition, they were still well -armed, in substantial fortifications and their senior officers were still making bellicose noises to anyone who cared to listen. Therefore, it was only sensible to prepare for the worst. In fact HQ Southern Command, who had been given the task of planning and conducting the operation to retake the islands, had been assuming the worst for some time – rather in the same manner as the Germans had done all those years before, when they had first planned to invade the islands – so those who expected to be involved in an assault were given a period of realistic training in and around the Brixham area of Devon, which it was felt most closely resembled the Channel Islands terrain. They also were trained in street fighting in the bombed areas of Plymouth. Despite these tough preparations, an

Brig Alfred Snow, OBE, commander of TF 135, was a tough no-nonsense 47 year-old ex-Somerset Light Infantryman. Here he is reading out the proclamation on the steps of Elizabeth College, Guernsey on 12 May 1945. IWM - HU 25970

138

alternative, 'softly, softly' approach was also planned for – and given the appropriate codename: 'Operation Omlette', in which small advance elements would be sent in to test the situation, again in the same way as the Germans had done, when Major Dr Albrecht Lanz and his men had; 'Fahren gegen Engeland!' Whatever the situation, however, there would still be the need for a fairly large force to disarm and take the garrision prisoner, then carefully check and demilitarise the islands, in order to remove the minefields and other dangers which abounded everywhere, especially along the coastlines.

The headquarters chosen to command the British relief force was HQ 115th Infantry Brigade, commanded by Brigadier Alfred Snow, OBE. It was shortly to be called: Task Force 135 (TF 135) and the operation became known as Operation NESTEGG. A 47-year old Somerset Light Infantryman, Snow had served during the latter stages of the Great War, then in India and Burma between the wars. He was appointed OBE in 1940 and took over command of the brigade in May 1943. 115 Infantry Brigade was a second-line Territorial Army Infantry Brigade and had been earmarked for posting to North West Europe until 4 July 1944 when its Brigade HQ was selected as TF 135. Initially the Task Force comprised both the infantry brigade, plus a number of artillery units, such as 127 HAA Regiment and a composite coast artillery regiment. They were put at seven days notice to move to the Channel Islands, but this was increased first to fourteen, then to twenty-eight. As 1945 began, it became clear that such a well-trained infantry formation should not be standing idle in UK while there was a continuing shortage of infantry in Northwest Europe, where the main battle against the Nazis was being fought. 115 Inf Bde was therefore removed from the Task Force and sent to fight in 21 Army Group, their place in TF 135 being taken by three artillery regiments – 614, 618 and 620 Artillery Regiments, RA, because as the need for artillery defence in the UK had lessened considerably, so artillery units became more readily available than infantry. The new 'infantry' brigade was given some hasty basic training and joined TF 135 as its main 'infantry' element. In his book; 'Liberated by Force 135' (see Bibliography), Mark Lamertion covers the organisation of TF 135 in considerable detail

TF 135 Shoulder Flash

and I recommend anyone interested in the liberation should obtain a copy.

TASK FORCE 135

In addition to a large Force HQ containing well over fifty staff officers and covering all staff branches including G, A & Q, Services, Hirings & Claims, Welfare, Movements, etc, there were the following major units:

RA Garrison (302 Inf Bde) comprising: 614 Regt, RA; 618 Regt, RA; 620 Regt, RA; 411 Indep HAA Bty, RA; No 1 Composite Coastal Unit, RA.

No 20 Civil Affairs Unit, with an HQ and sections for Jersey, Guernsey and Alderney.

Engineers: 158 CRE Works; 25 Stores Pl, RE; 82 Mech Egqpt Pl, RE; 1011 Port Op Coy, RE; 618 Fd Coy, RE, 259 Fd Coy, RE; 2 E & M Pl, RE; 223 Works Sec, RE, 224 Wks Sec, RE; 24 BD Pl, RE; Sec 964 PC & R Coy, RE.

Signals: 31 Tg Op Sec; Det 29 Med Wrls Sec; 4 Wrls Sec Type P; 110 Constr Sec; Force 135 Cipher Det; Det Force 135 Sig Sec; Force 135 Indep Sig Coy HQ.

Supplies & Transport: HQ 47 Tpt Coln, RASC; 230 Coy RASC (Inf Bde); 1758 Indep Amphibious Pl; 256 BIS; 841 Water Tpt Coy, 162 DID; A Sec 186 DID; M Sec Fd Bakery.

Medical: 209 Fd Amb (W); 79 Fd Hygiene Sec.

Ordnance: 135 Fd Ord Depot; 50 Mobile Bath Unit; AKS Exhibition Wing.

EME: 24 Port Wksp; Force 135 (LAD) Type A

Postal: 40 & 41 Indep Postal Units

Provost: 47(L) Inf Div Pro Coy, CMP.

Labour: 34 Coy Pnr Corps.

Intelligence: 159 FS Port Sec.

Movement Control: 135 MC Det

Pay: 8 Fwd Base Pay Office; 60 Area Cash Office; 169 Fd Cash Office

PW Camps: 801 PW Camp; 802 PW Camp; Force 135 Def Pl Royal Navy Det.

Royal Marines Det

Royal Air Force Det

PR Det

Static Marshalling Staff

(Source: Appendix XII 'Liberated by Force 135' – it also shows detail of dispositions as at May 1945)

Whilst the task and *raison d'etre* for these units should be clear from their designation, perhaps a word of explanation about tasks of No 20 Civil Affairs unit would be worthwhile. Their staff officers were responsible for all those aspects of civil administration necessary to get the islands going again. Thus in the run-up to the surrender they had collected and prepared for distribution a myriad of items which, it was felt, would be needed at once by the islanders. Top priority was given to food and clothing, with some 200 tons of essential supplies ready for immediate distribution, preloaded onto suitable transport. There were three months rations for the entire population, calculated to raise the the diet for each Islander to 2,750 calories a day (on a par with the rest of the UK), thereafter the normal food supply chain would take over. Clothing equal to fifteen months UK clothing ration was also brought, to be followed shortly by a further fifteen months supply. The food and clothing would be sold through the shops at prices similar to those currently charged in the UK. In addition, as a goodwill gesture from the British Government, was a free gift of luxuries such as chocolate, cigarettes and tobacco. They also stockpiled a large range of household and other goods – pots and pans, etc – doing their best to cover everything, even including a supply of morale boosting cosmetics for the women.

In the wardroom of HMS Bulldog on Wednesday, 9 May 1945. Kapitanleutant Armin Zimmerman is on the right of Generalmajor Siegfried Heine, Huffmeier's deputy. CIOS Jersey

Jersey. The Bailiff's pinnace on its way to HMS Beagle which was anchored in St Aubins Bay off St Helier. The Bailiff and Solicitor General waved their hats repeatedly, whilst Generalmajor Wulf and his two staff officers stood silent in the stern. Société Jersiaise

Liberation

By early May it became clear that Germany was in total collapse and that the liberation of the islands was imminent. It was thus necessary to bring TF 135 to a high state of readiness. SHAEF had alerted HQ Southern Command on 3 May and then two days later gave them permission to start negotiations, saying:

'Subject to you being satisfied as to the intention of the German Commander, Channel Islands, you should complete mounting and launch 'Nestegg' earliest practical date.'

Accordingly, all members of TF135 was ordered to assemble at Plymouth on 7 May 1945, together with their fully laden ships and landing craft. At the same time GOC in C Southern Command sent off a signal to Hueffmeier, saying that he was authorised to receive their unconditional surrender.

As might have been expected, from the fervent Nazi Vice-Admiral, he replied that he would only take orders from his own government. However, in the early hours of the 7th, word was received that the Germans had signed the unconditional surrender and that all hostilities would cease at midnight on 8 May. This was followed by a signal from Hueffmeier, which proposed that his representatives met the British reps four miles south of the Les Hanois light, to sign the surrender documents.

This was agreed, the time for the meeting being set at 1200hrs on Tuesday, 8 May 1945.

Two destroyers, HMS *Beagle* and HMS *Bulldog*, accordingly left Plymouth at 1000hrs, both carrying a landing party of two officers and twenty other ranks for each of the two main islands. Brigadier Snow was on HMS *Bulldog*, and the rendezvous was reached without a hitch. *Kapitanleutenant* Armin Zimmerman who was Hueffmeier's representative (postwar he would become the Inspector General for NATO) came on board the *Bulldog*, and told Brigadier Snow that he was authorised only to discuss the armistice and could not sign anything. He was told in no uncertain terms that he must return and prepare for unconditional surrender, but replied aggressively that the general cease-fire did not begin until midnight that night and if the destroyers did not withdraw from the RV they would run the risk of being shelled by the German coastal batteries. The Naval Force Commander, Rear Admiral C G Starr, had been ordered to avoid confrontation at all costs, so decided to withdraw out of range. A signal was then received to say that *Generalmajor* Siegfried Heine, commandant of Guernsey and Hueffmeier's deputy, would be at the RV at midnight and that he would be authorised to sign the surrender. This he did, arriving at the RV in a minesweeper, M4613 *Kanalblitz*, which had been used in mid-April for the German commando raid on the Cotentin peninsula. He signed eight copies of the surrender at 0114hrs on a rum cask on the quarterdeck of HMS *Bulldog*.

The destroyer then moved into St Peter Port and the Guernsey landing party went ashore, Lieutenant Colonel E G Stoneman, TD (CO of 618 Regt, RA) commanding, and accompanied by the head of the Civil Affairs Unit, Lieutenant Colonel H R Power, OBE, MC. Meanwhile Brigadier Snow had transferred to HMS *Beagle* and headed for Jersey, anchoring off St Helier and sending for Genmaj Wulf to sign the surrender of the island. Alexander Coutanche, the Bailiff, was asked to accompany him, together with the Island's Attorney General and the Solicitor General. On arrival Wulf was somewhat aggressive and arrogant, causing Brigadier Snow to express his severe displeasure in the most forthright language. This deflated the German completely and he signed the surrender without further ado. The formalities completed, it was time for the landing party, under Lieutenant Colonel William Robinson,

MC, (CO 620 Regt, RA), to disembark. He was accompanied by Capt Hugh Le Brocq, who had left Jersey in 1940 with the Royal Jersey Militia.

With the men of 620 Regt, RA, acting as Guard of Honour and the band of the DCLI in attendance, Lt Col Robinson, now Island Commander, acompanied by the Bailiff, Alexander Coutanche, made for the Royal Square for the Flag Hoisting Ceremony, then, later that day, Brig Snow read the Royal Proclamation in the same square, one historian commenting that: '... never has a ceremony of such historic importance to the island taken place in this little Square that took place at 1800hrs'. The Royal Proclamation read:

'People of the Channel Islands: It having pleased His Majesty by Order in Council to vest the officer commanding the armed forces in the Channel Islands all powers necessary for the success of our operation, the safety of our forces and the safety and well-being of his subjects in the Islands. I, Alfred Ernest Snow, as the officer commanding the forces give you greeting on your liberation from the enemy.

'I rely upon you all to work cheerfully and loyally to restore the normal life of your islands. Your ready compliance with such regulations and orders as may from time to time be issued by me or on my behalf will be in the best interests of the Islands. It will

Lt Col Robinson standing on the balcony of the Pomme D'Or Hotel, St Helier, surveying the happy crowd which had just watched the Union Jack being raised. Société Jersiaise

Alderney was liberated on 16 May 1945. Here Brig Snow and the British party talk to their counterparts at the German Naval Battery - Batterie Annes at La Giffoine, Alderney. CIOS Jersey

be my firm purpose to as to exercise my authority that your own Government may rapidly be restored to your Islands and that you may enjoy peace and prosperity your customary rights, laws and institutions.'

The military then gave the Royal Salute and, with heads bared, 'God Save The King' was sung lustily by all present. Brig Snow then read a letter from HM The King. The ceremony was concluded after Brig Snow had said a few words and the band of the DCLI had played several stirring marches.

'As the Brigadier and Admiral Stuart had walked down Hill Street during the afternoon, a slim, timid little girl detached herself from the crowd and shyly offered her hand to the Admiral. The tears sprang to his eyes and he promptly picked her up and kissed her. That we feel sure was meant for every little girl in Jersey.'[1]

What did Liberation mean?

It is not easy to put into words the feelings of the 'players' in this great drama, so let us leave it to three of them to try to express what it meant to each one of them. First, a member of the incoming victorious army, then a civilian and finally, one of the vanquished.

Op NESTEGG. This LST has come right up onto the beach to discharge its load in Guernsey.
La Valette Museum

'Bev' Bevins, Royal Engineers, was the driver of a heavy lorry in one of the 'Omlette' Groups that preceded the arrival of the main body. He recalled that his lorry was first off the landing craft: 'They sent me off first, I was the first lorry off the boat. They said, "Bevins, you go first. You've got 35 tons, so if you blow up they'll know we've arrived." I had got sandbags all around me. I could just move my feet and hands. And once ashore then our job was clearing mines that had been missed and God knows what. When we first landed it was hugs and kisses from the ladies; the men shook hands, patted our backs and asked if we had any cigs. We gave the children sweets; they thought it was Christmas. One thing sticks in my mind. I was standing by my lorry and the lads were clearing a Jerry store, making sure there were no booby traps, when this old lady came to me – it was lovely weather – with tears in her eyes and she said: "There you are, I said that an English soldier would have the first strawberry and you are he." And I had to stand there and eat it, and I cried with her.'[2]

Men of Task Force 135 greet the Channel Islanders, with sweets for the children. La Valette Museum

Some of the German garrison were made to work after surrender before going to PoW camps. Here a party dig up the railway tracks which they had laid in Jersey. <small>Société Jersiaise</small>

'Well, the liberation, you really had to be here to realise it' recalled Mr Ste Croix, who had been one of a party of dock workers bombed in St Helier harbour on Friday 28 June 1940,

'it's impossible to describe to anybody what liberation was like. You know when you've come out of the shadows like we had, where you're frightened to say this or you can't do this and all of a sudden all that drops away and you can go out and walk where you like and stay out. People don't realise, really it would do some of these people good to have an occupation because you can't walk down that street after nine o'clock at night and you can't talk over the garden wall to your neighbour because the woman across the road or the man across the street might be a little like that, that's the sort of situation that you find yourself in. And it's not a nice situation. And all of a sudden, all that falls and the feeling is, what's the word I could use? Exuberance, you're full, you're bubbling over.'[3]

And finally, a German soldier, Werner Wagenknecht, a medical sergeant, who had arrived on Guernsey in March 1942, one of a group of reinforcements to 319 Inf Div.

'A British officer escorted by soldiers came to our quarters a

Lines of PoWs were able to walk straight out to three LSTs (295, 521 & 527) which had been beached at St Aubin's Bay, Jersey, on 19 May 1945. (IWM - HU 5793)

few days after the capitulation. He wanted to see all the ambulances, medical equipment and our quarters. I had to give my last order for a roll-call. Whilst calling my comrades to attention, our little house-dog, a spaniel, who had lived with us in good times and had came to me in front of the unit, then "begged" in our direction and ran off – we were not ashamed to shed a few tears. I had to hand over all our belongings, burn our iron rations and pass over all the documents and service papers. The next day I reported to Elizabeth Hospital to be told that I would be supervising the embarkation of all the sick and wounded soldiers on 14 May onto a landing craft at St Sampson harbour – it was then that I saw how half-starved these men really were.

'My service in the German Army was now finished, but my friendship with Guernsey folks is still strong – we have happy relations with them, pay visits and speak to each other on the telephone.'

Notes

1. As quoted in *Liberated by Force 135* by Mark Lammerton.
2. Included on a tape made for the Tank Museum, Bovington.
3. Mr E J De Sainte Croix on IWM Dept of Sound Records Recording Accession No: 0010103/2

CHAPTER NINE

BRITISH COMMANDO RAIDS

The small size of the initial German garrision was an open invitation to the British to take some retaliatory action. Indeed this was advocated by Prime Minister Winston Spencer Churchill (WSC) as early as the 2 July 1940 when he wrote (in a note to his personal Chief of Staff, Major General Hastings Ismay):

> 'If it be true that a few hundred German troops have been landed on Jersey or Guernsey by troop carriers, plans should be studied to land secretly by night on the islands to kill or capture the invaders. This is exactly one of the exploits for which the Commandos would be suited.'

He goes on to comment that there should be no difficulty in getting information on the ground, etc from those who were evacuated from the Islands, and says that as the only way more reinforcements could reach the enemy during such fighting would be by aircraft carrier which would present an ideal opportunity for the RAF to bomb them. WSC closes his memo with the words: 'Pray let me have a plan.'

Operation AMBASSADOR and Operation ANGER
Guernsey 1940

The immediate reaction to the PM's memo was that Second Lieutenant Hubert Nicolle, late of the Guernsey Militia and now in the Hampshire Regiment, landed at le Jaonnet Bay on the south coast of Guernsey on 5 July. Despite the almost farcical beginning of his operation (it was reputed that he had to purchase his own folding canoe from Gamages, before going to Plymouth to board a submarine.) it was remarkably successful. He met up with two old friends who agreed to help him. One was his uncle, who was the assistant harbour master at St Peter Port, and was thus able to give him reliable information on the naval situation; whilst the other, a local baker who supplied bread to the Germans gave him the exact ration strength (469 all ranks) plus their locations – main body in St Peter Port with the rest manning machine gun posts around the island. His was only a reconnaissance mission which included checking on the suitability of the landing site for the main operation (to be codenamed: AMBASSADOR). He would be replaced by two more ex-Guernsey Militia who would then stay on the island and be ready to guide a large raiding party composed of No 3

John Durnford-Slater

Commando under Lieutenant Colonel John Durnford-Slater. This officer (later Brigadier, DSO and Bar) was in fact the very first commando soldier of the war, having been promoted from Captain to Lieutenant Colonel and chosen to raise and command No 3 Commando (Nos 1 & 2 did not at that time exist). As he explains in his autobiography:

'I had wanted action: I was going to get it. I should have been delighted to join at any rank, but was naturally pleased to get command. I was confident I could do the work and made up my mind to produce a really great unit.'

Back in Guernsey all was going well, the two new men (Second Lieutenant Philip Martel and Second Lieutenant Desmond Mulholland) arrived safely on the night of 9/10 July in the same manner as Nicolle via submarine and folding boat, and after he had briefed them, he rowed out to the submarine which had brought them to Guernsey, leaving them on the shore. Unfortunately from that moment onwards, everything started to go wrong. The raiders were due to arrive on the night of 12 July, meet their guides, assault the aerodrome burning aircraft, destroying fuel stocks, etc. However, bad weather delayed the operation for 48 hours during which time it was impossible to contact the two guides. After they had hidden for two days they returned to the beach, found no one there and nothing happening. They realised that something had gone seriously wrong so decided to steal a boat and try to get away, rather than putting their innocent families, who still lived on Guernsey, at risk. So, whilst they hid – first in a barn then in a house – near Vazon Bay, word was passed to Dame Sibyl Hathaway in Sark, whose son in law and daughter owned the house in which they were hiding, to ask for her help. She tells in her memoirs how she took some tinned supplies over to Guernsey, pretending to be in charge of her daughter's property. She met the two men who asked her if she could arrange for a fishing boat from Sark to pick them up, and she had the unenviable job of telling them that was impossible as the Germans guarded all the fishing boats very carefully. Also, it was impossible to get sufficient petrol. Despite this setback Martel and Mullholland managed to steal a boat at Perelle Bay – just west of Vazon Bay – but it was smashed to pieces on the rocks and they were left stranded. They would be forced to give themselves up before they could be rescued.

Whilst this drama was taking place, the main operation, Op AMBASSADOR, was suffering its own setbacks. In view of the 48 hour delay, the plan had to be amended. The original idea was for a force of forty men from 3 Commando, under Captain de Crespigny, to land first and create a diversion, whilst No 11 Independent Company attacked the airfield. This company would be split into two groups, the larger group of sixty-eight men, under Major Todd, would come ashore at Moye Point directly south of the airfield, whilst the rest of the company (another twenty men under Captain Goodwin) landed a mile or so further west. Two destroyers, HMS *Scimitar* and *Saladin* would transport them and escort seven RAF sea rescue launches (known as 'crash boats') that would take the men from ship to shore.

On the morning of 14 July, the intended day of departure, an officer sent from the Combined Operations Staff in London intercepted Durnford-Slater and told him that everything had changed, because they had discovered that the German garrision had been reinforced just where his commandos intended to land. Nothing daunted, a new plan was worked out on the spot, the force would now land at Petit Port on the south side of the island in Moulin Huet Bay, and departure was fixed for 1800 hours that evening. After completing all their preparations – assisted by some cadets from the Royal Naval College, Dartmouth, they set off on a lovely summer's evening. 'Lieutenant Joe Smale's party was to establish a roadblock on the road leading from the Jerbourg Peninsula to the rest of the island,' wrote Dornford-Slater in his autobiography, 'so that we would not be interrupted by German reinforcements. My own party was to attack a machine gun post and put the telegraph cable out of action. Captain de Crespigny was to attack the barracks situated on the peninsula and Second Lieutenant Peter Young was to guard the beach. Peter did not relish this job as he wanted more action. 'All right' I told him, 'if it's quiet come forward and see what's going on.'

As the party left harbour more problems began to occur. Two of the crash boats were found to be unfit and had to be left behind, which meant reorganising the loading details, transferring stores between boats and deciding that some of the crash boats would need to make at least two journeys inshore. The whaler of HMS *Scimitar* would also have to be used to ferry the commandos ashore. The convoy was about fifteen minutes late in starting and then was further delayed as one of the crash boats had to wait behind for stores and didn't then catch up until just before last light. It was a moonless night, so they did not see the Island until they were only some two miles away when the south coast suddenly appeared out of the gloom looking: '...dark and foreboding'. At about 0045 hours Durnford-Slater fortunately recognised the gap in the cliffs and was able to fix the place where they would climb up them. They clambered down rope netting on the side of their destroyer and boarded their launches in a calm sea. He comments: 'It was dead easy.'

However, the other party was not having such an easy time, having missed Guernsey completely and also having problems with the crash boats which were leaking badly. One of the commandos in this group was Sir Roland Swayne MC, then a young officer in the Herefordshire Regiment, who had been selected for commando training. His recollections of AMBASSADOR were recorded by the IWM Department of Sound Archives and he makes the point that it was the method of transportation which had let them down:

'It was beautifully planned from an army point of view but the naval preparation was very inefficient, partly due to inadequate equipment of course. ... it was a wonderful idea and it could have been a very, very clever raid. But the means of transport were absolutely hopeless. They towed gigs and whalers and I think the crash boats were towed – they may have gone under their own steam – but the gigs and whalers were towed by destroyers. Well, of course, it was much too fast for them and they got damaged going there. And when we got out from the destroyer into these boats they were all leaking. We decided to put into Sark and anyhow get rid of half the people on board so that there was a chance of this boat getting back to England

under its own steam. And we were making for Sark when the destroyer spotted us. Somebody on the destroyer – it was a soldier actually – spotted something in the water. He knew that there were people missing and he drew the attention of a ship's officer and he got the ship diverted to pick us up and we got home. It was very lucky we got home.'

Everything had also started to go wrong for Durnford-Slater. The pair of launches carrying his party had left the destroyer and set off on the agreed course, the naval officers in charge of the launches carefully watching their compasses rather than the coastline. Durnford-Slater soon realised that they were heading out to sea in the direction of France.

'"This is no bloody good", I said to the skipper of our launch, "we are going right away from Guernsey." He looked back and saw the cliff. "You're right! We are indeed. It must be this damned de-gaussing arrangement that's knocked the compass out of true. I ought to have it checked." "Don't worry about the compass," I said, "let's head straight for the beach!"

Thereafter they navigated by eye and were soon just about 100 yards from the shore. They had another scare when a large half-submereged rock was mistaken for an enemy submarine, but their real problems came when the boats, which did not have flat bottoms, grounded on rocks instead of smooth sand – their 48 hour delay having affected the state of the tide – so they had

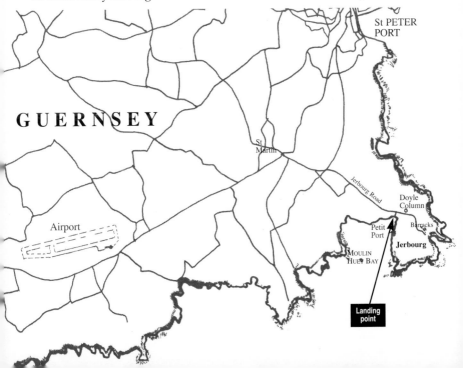

to jump out into armpit-deep water! They struggled ashore, with not a dry weapon amongst them and started to climb up a long flight of stone steps towards the houses at the top. As they reached them the neighbourhood dogs began to bark, but fortunately an Avro Anson aircraft began to circle right above them (this was part of the agreed cover plan) which helped to deaden the noise they were making. It worked! They reached the machine gun nest and the cable hut but found them both unoccupied. It was the same at the barracks – no one at home! Disappointed, they realised that they were now running well behind schedule, so decided to abort the mission and head for home. On the way down the steps, Durnford-Slater, who was at the rear, tripped and fell, his cocked revolver going off accidentally. This at last produced some reaction from the Germans, who started firing their machine guns out to sea, whilst the commandos were forming up on the beach to re-embark.

Getting away proved to be just as difficult. Because of the rocks, the launches could not get near enough and men and weapons had to be ferried out in one small dinghy, until it was dashed on the rocks and everyone had to swim for it. Somehow they managed to reach the launches and were pulled to safety. But the drama was not yet over. They were by now much later than had been anticipated, indeed the destroyers had already reluctantly decided to head for home, but the captain of HMS *Scimitar* made one last sweep and fortunately saw their frantic torch signals, came to the rescue and the bedraggled party was saved. All that is except for four men – Commandos Drain, Dumper, McGoldrick and Ross, who couldn't swim – what an admission for a commando to have to make. They were left behind, managed to evade capture for a few days, hoping to be picked up, but were eventually arrested while walking down the road to the aerodrome in broad daylight and finished the war in Stalag VIIIB in Upper Silesia. This of course still left Martel and Mulholland and so another Guernseyman in England, Stanley Ferbrache, volunteered to try to rescue them. He was taken over in an MTB and landed at La Jaonnet on 3 August, made contact with his uncle, Albert Callighan and his mother, Mrs Le Mesurier, who told him that the two men had already given themselves up to the German authorities the previous week. Ferbrache collected all the information he could (he is reputed as even walking around the airfield perimeter unchecked), and was safely taken off Guernsey on the night of 6 August.

That was the end of the ill-fated Operation AMBASSADOR. Sir Roland Swayne comments in his taped interview that it was a '... brave idea', but goes on to say:

'but we weren't remotely ready. We didn't know what kind of boats we wanted, we didn't know how to do it, there wasn't a proper planning body to prepare for these raids. In any case there was a fearful shortage of weapons and everything... we had no Tommy guns and we didn't have the Remington Colt which we were issued with later... we were armed with .38 revolvers which was, I always thought, a poor weapon. There was a shortage of ammunition for teaching the soldiers to shoot. Some of them had hardly done any practice on the range, it was all frightfully amateurish.'

Looking down at the beach at Petit Port, Guernsey (January 2002). July 15, 1940. Durnford-Slater slipped and fell on these steps accidently discharging his revolver.

His sentiments were echoed by the Prime Minister who was most displeased by the failure of Operation AMBASSADOR. He sent a scathing message to the HQ Combined Forces which included the words: 'Let there be no more silly fiascos like those perpetrated at Guernsey.' Next time they would have to do a great deal better – or else!

Operation DRYAD: Casquets – northwest of Alderney

After the fiasco of Operation AMBASSADOR it was vital that the next major British commando operation had to be a success and fortunately this was the case as far as Operation DRYAD was concerned. This would be undertaken by a new

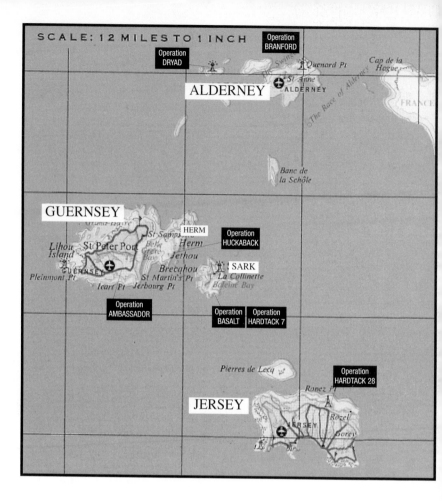

Special Service Unit, known as the Small Scale Raiding Force (SSRF), which was to be located at Anderson Manor in Dorset, not far from both Poole Harbour and the naval base at Portland, where its dedicated raiding boat MTB 344 was based. The Casquets Lighthouse was located on a dangerous chain of rocks some eight miles northwest of Alderney. The Germans had a seven-man crew there, supposedly keeping a constant visual and wireless watch, operating the light only when ordered to do so to help German convoys. The crew when Operation DRYAD took place had been there since 3 August 1942 and so was about halfway through their three month stint, probably therefore at the lowest point as far as morale, enthusiasm and efficiency was concerned, because for days on end they had seen neither ship

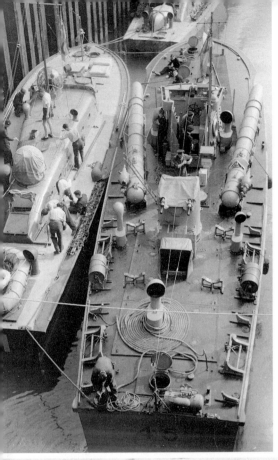

Op Ambassador. An RAF crash launch moored alongside an MTB, with another one just ahead. It shows clearly how much smaller they were, so no wonder they were damaged by a destroyer's wake when moving at speed.
IWM - A9921

Commandos drag the Goatley boat ashore. These lightweight wooden-bottomed, canvas-sided landing boats proved their worth during the attack upon the Casquets in September 1942.
IWM - H14593

nor aircraft. The 'highlight' of their tour so far had been the arrival, on 28 August, of an off-course carrier pigeon, carrying a message from an undercover agent in France to his 'spymaster' in UK, which was barely decipherable and was sent on to the *Hafenkommandanteur* in Cherbourg. On the night of 2/3 September 1942, a party of twelve men of the SSRF, under the command of Major Gus March-Phillips, DSO, landed on the Casquets, with the aim of taking prisoners, their role being aptly described in the phrase: 'the hand that plucks German sentries from their posts.' There had been some seven previous attempts to raid the Casquets lighthouse, but all had been abandoned through bad weather before they reached the rocks.

This time MTB 344 (affectionately known as 'The Little Pisser') with the SSRF party on board, sailed from Portland at 2100hrs and reached the Casquets at about 2245hrs, then managed to manoeuvre to within some 800 yards of the rock. Here the MTB was anchored and the landing party rowed ashore in a 'Goatley Boat' – a wooden-bottomed, canvas-sided landing boat which could carry ten men, weighed only 150kg, yet could be assembled in under two minutes by two men. The tricky currents meant it took some twenty minutes for them to reach the rocks just below the engine house tower. Successfully negotiating coiled dannert wire and a heavy 'knife-rest' of barbed wire, they reached the lighthouse complex, then, working to a carefully rehearsed plan, rushed the buildings and towers. They achieved complete surprise and there was no resistance, the entire seven man garrision being taken without a shot being fired. To quote from the SSRF report:

'Seven prisoners, all of them Germans, including two leading telegraphists, were taken in the bedrooms and living rooms. The light tower, wireless tower and engine room were all found to be empty, although the generating plant in the engine house was running, and the watch, consisting of two men was in the living room. The rest were in bed with the exception of two telegraphists who were just turning in. A characteristic of those in bed was the wearing of hairnets which caused to Commander of the party to mistake one of them for a woman.'

The raiding party and their prisoners now had to get back down the cliffs and re-embark. Some of the prisoners were still in their pyjamas, but time was getting short, so there was no chance of them changing into their uniforms. The wireless was smashed

Leaping ashore on training. Cap comforters have replaced steel helmets. This is the sort manoeuvre that must have taken place when landing on the Casquets. Philip Ventham

up with an axe, the building searched for useful documents, all the weapons and ammunition (including an Oerlikon cannon and two large cases of grenades) were dumped into the sea. Then the SSRF party plus their prisoners re-embarked onto the Goatley which coped magnificently with a total of nineteen men instead of the usual maximum of ten. Despite a rising sea, the MTB reached Portland safely at about 0400hrs. The captured material – signal books, wireless log, papers and personal photographs etc, were then passed on to higher authority. The Germans did not discover that their garrision was missing for a number of days, but when they did so, they immediately strengthened the lighthouse crew to over thirty and provided more weapons including a 2.5cm Pak gun, five machine-guns, more hand grenades, etc. They also built extra defences – putting in more barbed wire entanglements, trip wires and mines. However, the Casquets were never again raided, the crew of two officers and thirty-six men eventually being taken prisoner on 17 May 1945 after the surrender.

OPERATION REPORT

M.T.B. 344 and 10 officers and 2 O.Rs. of S.S.R.F. personnel took part. The M.T.B. sailed from Portland Bill at 21.00 hrs. Wednesday 2nd September, 1942. In spite of a very careful overhaul, the port engine again gave trouble and the passage had to be made at a reduced speed of some 25 knots for the first 25 miles. It was then possible to increase the engine revolutions, and the normal cruising speed of 33 knots was maintained until within five miles of the objective.

At 22.30 hrs. speed was reduced to 15 knots, and a red light flashing one every fifteen seconds was seen very fine on the port bow. This was at first believed to be the CASQUETS, but at 22.45 hrs. a rock was reported on the port beam at about one mile rise, and course was altered to close with it. This turned out to be the CASQUETS, and course was laid to approach it from the Northward against the tide, the M.T.B's. main engines were then cut off and the silent auxiliary used. The red light was identified as SARK.

The M.T.B. was manoeuvred to within 800 yards of the rock, where she was anchored with a 45lb. Admiralty pattern anchor and 50 fathoms of 2½ inch rope, and the landing party went ashore in a Goatley pattern assault craft paddling four aside, and leaving the M.T.B. at 00.05 hrs.

Unlike plans made for previous occasions, the landing was made, not at any recognised landing point, but on the face of the rock immediately under the engine house tower. This was done partly because of the difficulty of finding holding ground for the kedge anchor on the recognised North landing, and partly because it was feared that the landing points might be guarded or set with booby traps. There was a fairly heavy run on the rocks from the South Westerly swell, but the kedge anchor held well and the landing was made without mishap or any harm being done to the boat. A way was then found up the 80 ft. cliff, and any noise made by the party was drowned by the rumble of the surf and the heavy booming of the sea in the chasms and gulleys.

Coiled Dannert wire was met and climbed through on the way up the cliff, and the gateway was found to be blocked by a heavy knife rest barbed wire entanglement, but way was found over the Western wall and the whole party made the courtyard unchallenged. At this point the order was given for independent action and the party split up and rushed the buildings and towers, according to a pre-arranged plan. Complete surprise was obtained and all resistance overcome without a shot being fired.

Seven prisoners, all of them Germans, including two leading telegraphists were taken in the bedrooms and living rooms. The light tower, wireless tower and engine room were all found to be empty. A characteristic of those in bed was the wearing of hairnets, which caused the Commander of the party to mistake one of them for a woman.

The prisoners were re-embarked immediately, and taken down over the rocks by the way the raiding party had come up, some of them still in their pyjamas. The wireless was then broken with axes, and the buildings and offices searched for papers, documents and code books. The light and the engine room was left intact. The following papers were removed:-

Code book for Harbour Defence Vessels F.O.i/c France
Signal and Log Books
Records and W/T Diary
Procedure Signals
Personal letters and photographs
Identity books, Passes and Ration Cards.

These papers were handed over to the Military Authorities at Portland on return.

A thorough search of the buildings revealed the presence of a quantity of arms and ammunition. Each man was equipped with a rifle of the old Steyr pattern and there were two large cases of stick grenades, one of them open. There was also an Oerlikon cannon-shell (small calibre) gun, loaded and placed against the wall in the living room. If a good watch had been kept, or if any loud noises had been made on the approach or landing, the rock could have been rendered pretty well impregnable by seven determined men.

G. MARCH-PHILLIPPS. Major S.S.R.F.

Operation BASALT – Sark

A few days after DYRAD a small number of SSRF landed on the island of Burhou, some three miles northwest of Alderney. This operation, codenamed BRANFORD was little more than a reconnaissance and search mission and they left after finding nothing. Operation BASALT was, however, very different indeed. It took place on 3 October 1942, the aim being to capture prisoners and recconoitre the German defences on Sark. The twelve-strong party under Major Geoffrey Appleyard, landed safely close to Point Chateau, having persuaded the German lookout post on Little Sark that they were a German E-boat needing to shelter in Dixcart Bay. The raiders made their way up the steep cliffs, cut through barbed wire, hid from a German patrol

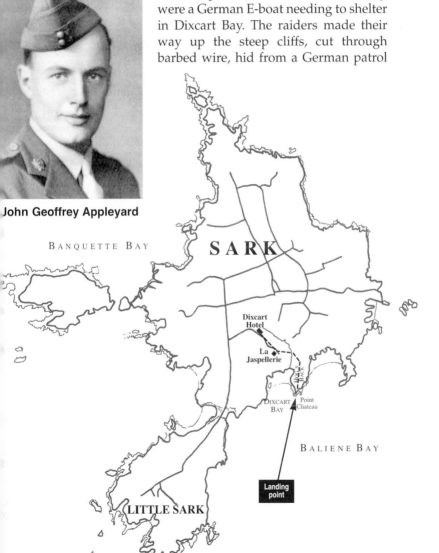

John Geoffrey Appleyard

BANQUETTE BAY

SARK

Dixcart Hotel

La Jaspellerie

DIXCART BAY

Point Chateau

BALIENE BAY

Landing point

LITTLE SARK

Aerial view of Dixcart and La Jaspellerie Tenement with cliff paths leading to the bay. J Brannam

and eventually reached the Dixcart Hotel which was being used by the Germans. They made a noisy entrance, took five men of an engineer detachment who were fast asleep in bed, prisoner, tying their hands behind their backs. However, they failed to gag their prisoners, who, having recovered from their initial shock, began shouting and creating a rumpus whilst the commandos were searching the rest of the premises. A running battle developed as the Germans tried to escape, resulting in two of the prisoners being shot dead, two getting away – one of whom was stark naked the other wounded, leaving the raiders with just one prisoner. Taking him with them the commandos set off for the cliffs with the Germans in hot pursuit. Fortunately the MTB was still waiting for them despite it being far later than the time agreed and the party was able to row out to the MTB and make good their escape.

Naturally the divisional commander, *Generalmajor* Mueller was furious and ordered both the Island Commander (*Oberleutnant* Herdt) and the orderly NCO to be court martialled. The *Geheime Feldpolizei* also began a series of lengthy

B A S A L T

SUMMARY OF OPERATION AND ITS SEQUEL.

This small and completely successful operation may be
summarized by saying that on the night of the 3rd October a
party of 12 officers and O'R's landed from M.T.B. 344 at Pointe
Chateau, Sark, reconnoitred various places on the island and
collected documents, and surprised five Germans in their beds in
the Annexe of Dixcart Hotel.   Four attempted to escape from their
captors, who had already been reduced in number by the boat guard etc.
Those who made this attempt were all shot, and - so far apparently as
was known to the Force Commander, Major J.C. Appleyard, M.C., - fatally
shot.   The remaining prisoner was brought off, along with several
documents of interest.   Here, so far as the British were concerned,
the affair was closed, as there was no intention to publish any account
of it.

Unfortunately, however, at least one of the prisoners had succeeded in escaping.   This fact was announced in a German communiqué of
three days later, a copy of which is among the attached papers.   The
German High Command declared that the men had been illegitimately roped
and that it was while resisting this that two had been shot, and treated
this alleged barbarity as a sequel to similar alleged barbarity at
Dieppe.   In the midst of a storm of libellous allegations against the
Allies - extending from the employment of prisoners to clear mines in
the Mediterranean, and the shooting of shipwrecked soldiers in the
Levant, through the gagging and binding of/German prisoner taken on the
Lofoten Islands and the machine-gunning of some first aid units of the
Folgare Division, besides other Libyan atrocities, down to keeping
Japanese in prisoners of war camps on the cold ground - they announced
the shackling of all officers and men taken at Dieppe.   Upon this
C.O.H.Q. published an account of the raid, adding certain details as
to the forced deportation of the inhabitants of Sark (copy annexed).
On the 9th Berlin announced that 1376 British Officers and O.R's had
been put in fetters.   On the 10th the British Government made a further announcement (copy annexed).   A number of points were now brought
into controversy, such as how far a distinction could be drawn between
what may be done in the course of battle and what may be done after
the prisoner is in safe custody, and whether there were any barracks
on the island.   These points are more germane to this operation than
the larger question of the shackling of prisoners generally, as to
which it need only be recalled that, after 1376 German prisoners had
been manacled in Canada, their chains were taken off on December 12th
on the proposal of the Swiss Government that this should be done
simultaneously by both belligerents, but that the German Government
refused to release their prisoners until a further demand made by them
was satisfied, that the British Government would give an assurance forbidding the binding or shackling of prisoners in any circumstances
whatever (vide e.g. Mr. Eden's speech in Evening Standard of April 21st,
1943).

SUMMARY OF OPERATION AND ITS SEQUEL (contd)

escape, and no greater severity than was necessary to prevent this is even alleged by the German Government. The further statement that the prisoners had to be taken past a German occupied barracks was denied on the ground that there were no barracks. This may have been the case in the strict sense of the word, but there were certain a number of troops billeted in various places on this small island. The total number of Germans was believed to be 300 according to the Intelligence received.

One result of the publication of this raid by Berlin was the publication on the British side of the two proclamations given or summarized in the Daily Mirror of October 8th, and the Guernsey Star of September, 26th, (the latter through the News of the World of October 11th, 1942,) regarding deportation from the Channel Islands; the P.W's statement revealing that the object was conscription for for labour.

An underlying contributory cause of the great to-do made by the German High Command over this incident was the fact that it chafed un the necessity of subtracting a disproportionate quantity of defensive armament and troops to deal with what it styled "Red Indian raids" which had nothing to do with the main theatre of war, and possibly trusted to bring the commando nuisance to an end by a combination of ridicule and shrecklichkeit.

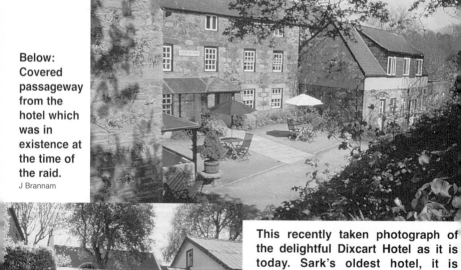

Below:
Covered
passageway
from the
hotel which
was in
existence at
the time of
the raid.
J Brannam

This recently taken photograph of the delightful Dixcart Hotel as it is today. Sark's oldest hotel, it is located high up a suntrapped valley and was converted from from a 16th Century feudal farm 'longhouse'. The perfect place for a secluded holiday.
J Brannam

interrogations and for weeks the Islanders lived in fear of reprisals. The German propaganda machine then seized on the fact that two of the prisoners had been shot with their hands tied behind their backs, stridently accusing all commandos of acts of barbarism. This led Combined Operations HQ into taking the unusual step of publishing a brief account of the raid in which it was claimed that the purpose had been to obtain first-hand information about the suspected ill-treatment of British residents on the Island. This they said was confirmed by the fact that a proclamation by FK515 had been seized, which ordered all male civilians between the ages of 16 and 70 who had not been born in the Channel Islands or who were not permanent residents, to be deported to Germany, together with their families. This was of course true, however, it had not really been the main reason for mounting the raid.

It also caused Adolf Hitler, who was beside himself with rage about the whole incident, to order that all British prisoners taken during the Dieppe raid (launched 19 August 1942) were to be shackled. This led to 'tit-for-tat' shackling of unfortunate prisoners on both sides which threatened to get out of control until the Swiss authorities took a hand as mediators and persuaded both sides to unfetter all prisoners simultaneously. However, it also prompted the Fuehrer to issue an order in October 1942, to all his commanders, giving them *carte blanche* to execute any commandos who might be captured in any future raids:

    ' ... in uniform or not ... whether in battle or escaping ... to be destroyed to the last man.'

This was perhaps a measure of how upset he was that his 'Mailed Fist of the Atlantic Wall' could be penetrated so easily by miniscule raids of the SSRF and other Allied commandos.

Operation HUCKABACK – Herm

1943 saw its fair share of commando activity, including small operations like one against St Peter Port harbour, on the night of 8/9 January, when an attempt was made to attach limpet mines to ships in the harbour, but it had to be aborted due to appalling weather. Then on the night of 27/28 February, there was a successful recce of the tiny island of Herm, to see if it would be a suitable location for supporting artillery in the event of a full-scale landing on Guernsey. This was a small raid of just

Combined Operations Headquarters,
1A Richmond Terrace,
Whitehall, S.W.1.

4th March, 1943.

Copy No. 27.

S.R. 1272/43.

ENCLOSURE "C"

Report on Operation HUCKABACK.

M.T.B. reached its anchorage at approximately 2245.
The anchorage was about half a mile from the landing point, there
was a slight northerly tide which decreased on closing shore.

2.   The landing place chosen was in the small bay 200
yards to the north-west of SELLE ROCKS. · The landing was made
quite easily on a large-size shingle beach.   As soon as
Force Commander and leading Scout were ashore, a reconnaissance
was made of the cliffs surrounding the cove. These cliffs
are about 100 ft. high, and are composed of soft clay.   Three
attempts were made to scale the cliffs on the north side of
the cove, but were unsuccessful.   An ascent was finally
made up the bed of a small stream which comes in, in the
middle of the western cliff.   Force Commander carried a rope
up this cliff, and pulled remainder of force up.   A sentry
was left at the top of the cliff.

3.   The force then moved up along a wall which runs
approximately north from landing place.   The fields were
rough pasture land, and on them, going was easy.   On the
seaward side of the wall, there was a certain amount of low
scrub and brambles, which made movement extremely noisy.
Fields were divided up by low stone walls which were very easy
to climb.   Force continued northwards to the small patch of
wood due east of BELVOIR HOUSE, where a reconnaissance was
made by Force Commander.   There seemed to be no sign of activity
and the ground all round the house was very overgrown ...
Lt. Thompson and two men took up covering positions round the
house.   Capt. Porteous and three men forced an entry into
the house and searched the building, which was completely
deserted and unfurnished.   There were no signs of footmarks in
the dust which was lying thickly over everything.   While the
house was being searched, Capt. Hewitt, accompanied by one man,
made a reconnaissance of BELVOIR Beach and of the route from
the beach inland.

4.   The Force then reformed and moved westwards along
a wall from BELVOIR HOUSE until striking the track beside the
Chateau.   During this stage the Force was ambushed by a
sheep which could be heard moving in some thick undergrowth.

5.   The Force moved northwards along the track which was
fairly well metalled and capable of carrying fairly heavy
transport.   A permanent wire fence had been put up across the
road about 100 yards north of the Chateau.· From here on, the
road did not appear to have been used recently as there were
bushes and brambles growing across it.   Force continued to
the fork between North-west hill and North hill;   thence along
a sandy track across the golf-course to the northern end of
SHELL BEACH.   There was no sign of any enemy activity in this
part of the island, no mines or wire or weapon-pits were seen.
The golf-course was very overgrown with brambles and rushes.
The ground in this area is all sandy, covered with turf, and it
would be possible to drive wheeled or tracked vehicles without
difficulty.

/6....

ten men led by Captain P A Porteous VC. This officer had been awarded the Victoria Cross after the landings at Dieppe in August 1942, for pressing on with an attack against enemy guns despite being wounded in the arm and hand. The party covered the island over a three hour period and saw no obvious signs of German occuaption.

Another raid on Herm on the night of 3-4 April, to take a prisoner had to be aborted due to bad weather.

atrick Anthony Porteous

Operation HARDTACK 28 – Jersey

Jersey was now the only important island not to have been raided, so Operation HARDTACK 28 (one of a series of pre-D Day raids on the Channel coast) was carried out in late December 1943. The small party of ten commandos from the 2nd Special Boat Section arrived by a motor gun-boat and landed safely at Petit Port on the northern coastline. They proceeded to exit the beach by the steep path until they came to a barbed wire fence upon which was secured a board warning of mines. They had just walked the length of a minefield and come off unscathed; the return journey would be different story. Further up the

Philip Atterbury Ayton

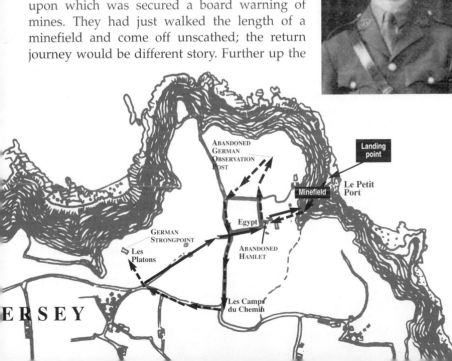

Looking out to sea from Petit Port beach, Jersey, where the Commandos came ashore. The beach has changed little in the last sixty years. Michael Ginns

Looking inland from Petit Port beach showing the route the Commandos took. Michael Ginns

Resistance Nest Jasmin at Les Platons which the Commandos were unable to gain access. In the undergrowth behind the buildings are neglected trenches, MG positions and mortar pits constructed during the occupation. The buildings today house the telecommunication systems for the States of Jersey Harbours and Airport. Michael Ginns

Coastal artillery observation post M5, which the Commandos found locked and deserted. In fact the Germans never used it as it was in the middle of their Kampfbahn (battle training ground). The aerials are to do with radiation monitoring because of the French nuclear power station 25-30 miles across the sea. Michael Ginns

path was an abandoned hamlet which was used by the Germans for training and also served as a target for artillery. From there they moved north towards the headland where a German post was believed to be situated. However, this observation post proved to be abandoned. They decided upon the bold step of marching down the road towards Les Camps du Chemin – they decided that should anyone see or hear them they would be taken for a German patrol. They called at two houses and knocked up a frightened lady who directed them to a nearby farm where, she insisted, they would get any information they required. At the farm the Le Breton brothers received the commandos and imparted some useful information concerning the enemy's strength and disposition of troops. Further, they volunteered to lead the raiding party to the nearby strongpoint just up the road at Les Platons.

By the time the commandos had reached the perimetre wire surrounding the strongpoint, which was garrisoned by twenty-five men, it was noted that they were running out of time and the party made its way back to the pick-up place at Petit Port. Whilst negotiating the wire fence leading down to the beach Captain Philip Ayton stepped on a mine and was seriously wounded. The rest of the party managed to carry him down the cliffs into the dory and safely out to the Motor Gun Boat (MGB), without the Germans being alerted. They reached England safely, but he however died on the following day in hospital.

One of the ruined houses in Egypt. This deserted village was used as a training ground by the Germans.
Michael Ginns

This ground was where the minefield was and the memorial to Captain Ayton is located on the spot where he was fatally wounded. Michael Ginns

Schoolchildren gather here for a ceremony, along with members of the Royal British Legion and Les Anciens Combattants Francaises, on the Friday before Remembrance Sunday.

Operation HARDTACK 7 – Sark

The final commando raid on the Channel Islands was also called HARDTACK – HARDTACK 7 in this case, and timed to coincide with HARDTACK 28. The target was Sark and the raiding party under Lieutenant McGonigal landed on the most southerly point of Derrible Point just after midnight on Christmas Day. Unfortunately it soon became clear that there was a sheer, unclimable ridge between the Point and the mainland, so they returned to the dory after carefully reconnoitering another landing place in Derrible Bay. Having made sure there were no mines on the beach or in the cliff area, they rejoined their MGB and returned to Portland. Two nights later they returned to Derrible Point, landed safely and, taking a similar route to the Operation BASALT raiders (of 3 October 1942), headed inland to capture a prisoner. However, this was foolish as they should have realised that the Germans would have increased their minefields in the area after Operation BASALT. As they were moving slowly along, with those in front feeling for mines, two exploded at the rear of the party, killing one man and severely wounding another. They realised that they must all be inside a minefield. As they were endeavouring to get their casualties out of the minefield, two more mines went off at the front of the party, wounding McGonigal and killing another member of the patrol. More mines then went off around them and they may have come under heavy machine gun fire (this was never confirmed and they never actually saw any enemy during the raid). They decided to abort the mission, but had to leave behind the two dead commandos (both Frenchmen) and some of their equipment including a wireless set and some scaling ropes. Nevertheless, they got to the MGB without further incident and reached Portland safely. This was the last of the commando raids on the Channel Islands.

The final commando operation against the islands was Op Hardtack 7, when commandos raided Sark. IWM - H 17485

170

CHAPTER TEN

EXPLORING THE ISLANDS

So much to see

Although the Channel Islands were mercifully spared many of the usual scars of warfare, they are nevertheless covered with an evocative tapestry of strange wartime buildings – some of which are unique to the islands – and also with associated tunnels and earthworks. Some of these buildings have been restored so that, as far as possible, they can be viewed as they were when in use during the Occupation. It can be argued that all such buildings should be razed to the ground and that all mention of them expunged from the Islands' history, yet the Castles and Martello towers of earlier periods of warfare, are readily accepted by all as 'proper' historical monuments. One cannot be selective as far as history is concerned, therefore I fully support the aims and ambitions of the members of the Channel Islands Occupation Society, both the Jersey and Guernsey Branches, who seek to discover and record all that remains of the Occupation and to restore where possible those buildings of special interest. Inevitably such sites become places of great interest to both local people and to the visitors who flock to these delightful holiday islands. Some, alas, seek to pour scorn on such work, claiming that money is being made by fostering the despised Nazi culture. I think this is both a dangerous and small-minded view. Those who seek to bring history to life, be it via a *bona fide* museum collection or by authentic restoration, should be applauded – *always provided* they go for fact and not fiction and do not glorify the Third Reich and all it stood for, but rather try to tell the story of the Occupation truthfully, as I hope that I have done, warts and all.

Getting there

Both Guernsey and Jersey have excellent airports and harbours, so there are no problems travelling to these holiday islands from anywhere in the world, however, obviously the most frequent services both by sea and air, are from the UK. Any travel agent will have full details, which can also be obtained on the net. Air *Aurigny* operate a fifteen minute flight from Guernsey to Alderney's small airport, or there is a 20 mile sea crossing. Sark, and the other small islands can be reached by boat.

Where to stay

As there is so much to see, the would-be Second World War historical 'explorer' needs to be properly prepared and to have worked out a suitable itinerary. Whilst the locations and details of some sites have already been explained, I have tried in this final chapter, to give a brief resumé of the most important sites, museums, etc which are there to be visited on each of the islands, while the Bibliography contains a useful selection of books about the subject. None of the islands are very large, and the main ones have excellent road networks. NB There are speed restrictions on ALL roads in Alderney, Guernsey and Jersey, and cars are not permitted on Sark, which means that everywhere is readily accessible. Being much visited holiday islands, they have excellent, highly experienced tourist organisations from whom you can obtain a mass of useful material. They also have a wide range of excellent hotels, boarding houses and camp sites, etc, so there is masses of accomodation to choose from. The best initial contact addresses are:

States of Guernsey Tourist Board.
PO Box 23, St Peter Port, Guernsey, Channel Islands GY1 3AN
(Information Centre)
Tel: (+44) (0) 1481 726611;
Fax: (+44) (0) 1481 721246;
email: enquiries@tourism.guernsey.net www.guernseytourist-board.com

Jersey Tourism.
Liberation Square, St Helier, Jersey JE1 1BB
(Information Centre
Tel: (+44) (0) 1534 500700;
Fax: (+44) (0) 1534 500899;
email: info@jersey.com www.jersey.com

The Channel Islands Occupation Society

The leaders in the study of the years of German occupation are the Channel Islands Occupation Society, which has separate branches in Guernsey (covering also Alderney, Sark and the smaller islands) and in Jersey. The main aims of the Society are twofold:

a. to study and investigate the German Occupation of the Channel Islands.

b. to further interest in the Occupation by recording, safeguarding and preserving relics and monuments of the period.

Ever since 1973, the two branches have taken it in turns to publish a yearly review (Guernsey in even years, Jersey in odd); publish regular newsletters, pamphlets on relevant subjects, organise tours, excursions and talks on relevant subjects. Anyone who is seriously interested in the subject is strongly advised to join the Society and should write to one of the two secretaries, who are just now:

Guernsey
Maj (Retd) E. Ozanne
Les Jehans Farm
Torteval
GUERNSEY GY8 0RE
(tel: 01481 64625)

Jersey
Mr W M Ginns, MBE
'Les Geonnais de Bas'
St Ouen
JERSEY JE3 2BS
(tel: 01534 482089)

The CIOS include a word of warning on 'bunker hunting' in each of their yearly reviews, which contains sound common-sense and should be followed by anyone exploring on their own. It reads:

'Most of the bunkers, gun pits and defences are on private property. If you want to have a look, obtain permission from the owner. Do not enter without a strong torch or lamp. There are different designs of defences that from the outside look the same, but once inside, passages may descend without warning. Also, wellington boots may be needed as 50-plus years of dirt and dust will have blocked the drains. We would warn you that bunkers on the coast will also have been

CAUTION

This headland is crossed by German field defences (including trenches), and some parts of the headland have recently been made unstable by coastal erosion. Members of the public who choose to use this area do so entirely at their own risk.

Danger Notice. This is the sort of problem to be faced by the would-be 'bunker hunters'.
Alec Forty

173

used as unofficial toilets – so beware! Young persons should not
enter without an adult, as many bunkers have awkward steps
and hidden ducts that can trap the unwary. Bunkers and tunnels
have been blocked up for this reason and no other; those of you
who would like to find an Aladdin's Cave of war relics have been
beaten to it by the scrap drive of 1947-48.'

Museum Services

Both Guernsey and Jersey have excellent Museum Services
which can be the source of a considerable amount of relevant
material, for example, the Guernsey Museums and Art Gallery
at Castle Cornet and Fort Grey. These are administered by the
States of Guernsey Heritage Committee

However, as they cover the entire history of Guernsey, only a
proportion of their exhibition space is devoted to the German
Occupation. Archive material, photographs and copies of parts
of *Festung* Guernsey[1] are housed in the Royal Court Library and
the Prialux Library. Jersey Museum Service also run museums
in which sections are devoted to the German Occupation, such
as Elizabeth Castle, St Helier. Working in cooperation with the
Jersey Museum Service is the Société Jersiaise, which holds a
significant photographic archive.

Introductory Video

Without doubt the Tomahawk Films 'Living History' video
entitled *Channel Islands Occupied* is a splendid introduction to
any visit and includes rare captured wartime newsreels. Its running time is 50 minutes and it is available via: Brian Matthews,
No 3 Dolphin Hill, Twyford, Winchester, SO21 1PU (Tel: 01962
714989)

Getting about

SUNFLOWER BOOKS of 12, Kendrick Mews, London SW7
3HG, produce excellent small pocketsized guide books written
by Geoff Daniel, in their *Sunside Countryside Guide* series,
which, in addition to containing much information about the
islands, give suggested car tours, long and short walks,
suggested picnic locations, etc. However, these are naturally for
general visitors and not specifically orientated for military
enthusiasts. Harper Collins Publishers Ltd produce colour
Holliday Maps of the islands under the Collins imprint, which

also contain much useful general information, whilst there is a plethora of leaflets available for all the main places of interest.

The *German Occupation of Jersey Map* is, without a doubt, the very best map as far as the details of the occupation of Jersey is concerned. Mr Howard B Baker's highly detailed map, which can be bought at most bookshops on Jersey, is priced around £2. As well as cramming the map with useful information he has written on its back, a comprehensive history of the war years on the island, which is the result of considerable detailed research – so you really do get good value for money!

GUERNSEY – MAIN SITES OF INTEREST

Fortress Guernsey issues (free) a very useful little leaflet which covers their most important sites. These are:

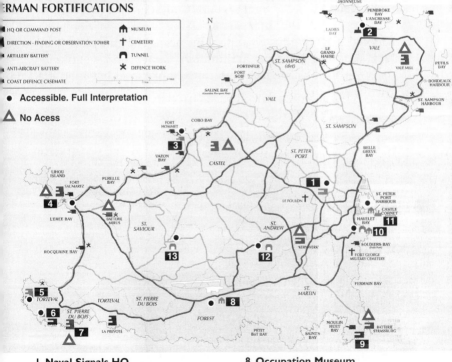

1. Naval Signals HQ
2. L'Ancresse Flak Battery
3. Fort Hommet Casemate
4. L'Erée Trenches
5. Pleinmont Tower
6. Batterie Dollmann
7. L'Angle Tower

8. Occupation Museum
9. Observation Posts
10. Underground Hospital
11. Castle Cornet
12. Underground Hospital
13. St. Saviour's Tunnels

RESTORED SITES

Naval Signal Headquarters. This comprises a complex of three large concrete bunkers in the grounds of the La Collinette Hotel which housed the German Naval HQ for the Islands. The bunker was completed in 1944 and has been well preserved, retaining all of its original fittings. It has now been carefully refurbished and re-equipped to tell the story of wartime naval signals. Parking is available at the Beau Sejour Centre.

The Naval Signal Headquarters. Entrance to the three-bunker complex in the grounds of the La Collinette Hotel. Inside it has been fully restored.
Alec Forty

Coast Defence Casemate. One of the four casemates at Fort Hommet, which formed the principal armament of this important infantry strongpoint (Stutzpunkt Rotenstein), and is one of 21 'fortress' bunkers built on Guernsey to house 10.5cm K 331(f) guns. Meticulously restored to its original condition (including the gun, crew quarters, entrance defence, ammunition stores and ventilation room), it forms a perfect time capsule of the Occupation era. Nearby parking.

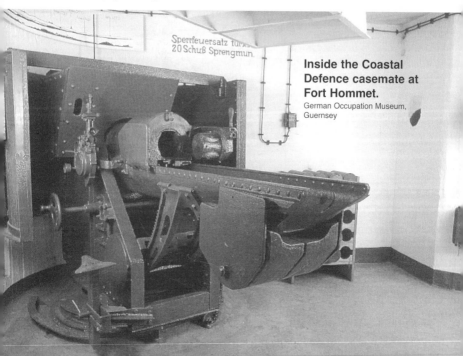

Inside the Coastal Defence casemate at Fort Hommet.
German Occupation Museum, Guernsey

Pleinmont Direction-finding Tower (MP3) at L'Eree.Inside the Pleinmont Tower, the crew standby room has been faithfully restored as it was when an NCO and four/five men manned it. Note the escape hatch on the right of the chimney.
Author's Collection

Pleinmont Tower. This Direction-finding Tower (MP3), one of those which are unique to the Channel Islands was built in 1942 and the adjoining personnel shelter the following year. Built to provide elevated direction-finding positions to control the fire of the heavy coastal batteries, this tower has five observation levels and a platform mounted radar unit was mounted on the roof. It has now been carefully restored with an interpretation centre in the adjoining shelter, it contains items of original equipment and offers wonderful coastal views. Nearby parking.

Battery Dollmann. Covering an extensive area on the head-land at Pleinmont, this Army coastal artillery bat-tery of four French 22cm guns in open emplace-ments with extensive sup-porting installations, was one of the earliest of the permanent defences estab-lished in 1941. A continu-ing careful restoration pro-gramme is in hand and one of the four gunpits can now be visited together with trenches linking it with its two magazines. Nearby parking.

Battery Dollmann, the photo shows one of the clifftop observation posts.
Alec Forty

177

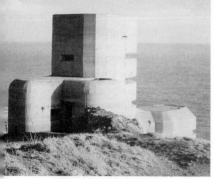

L'Angle Tower. Massive direction-finding tower, looking like the bridge superstructure of a battleship. Alec Forty

LISTED SITES

L'Angle Tower. Looking like the bridge superstructure of a battleship, this remarkable direction-finding tower was built high on the cliffs to control a battery of naval coastal artillery that was never installed. At the end of the occupation it had been fitted with a gun laying radar used as part of a chain of more sophisticated fire-control equipment at the disposal of German naval artillery units.

Flak Battery Dolmen. This was the site of six 8.8 cm Flak guns near L'Ancresse Bay. Alec Forty

Flak Battery Dolmen. The powerful Anti-Aircraft defences of Guernsey were an essential support for the ground defences on Guernsey. Located on rising ground to the west of L'Ancresse Bay are the emplacements for six Flak 8.8cm guns, plus adjoining shelters, command bunker and radar. One of six similar batteries, this site was constructed with permanent concrete installations that could also command the seaward approaches to the north of the island. Parking nearby.

Observation Posts. On the coastal path at Jerbourg, with

178

Observation Posts. These small, concrete OPs are located at Jerbourg with commanding views to the south. Alec Forty

commanding views to the south and over to a distant Jersey, lie two distinctive concrete observation posts that were built in 1941, along with a number of others around the coast. These advanced positions supplied fire-control information to the Army coastal batteries inland. A third temporary position lies in front of the battery command post at the head of the path leading down to St Martin's Point. Parking nearby.

Castle Cornet. 800 years of history are to be found here, including additional fortifications built by the Germans. Alec Forty

Castle Cornet. With a history spanning over eight hundred years it now houses several first class museums which tell the story from prehistoric times to the present day. During the German occupation, additional fortifications were constructed and a number of bunkers and gun emplacements remain. Refreshments and WCs available.

Trench System. One of the first tasks of TF 135 after liberation in May 1945, was to clear away the defensive fieldworks which surrounded many German strongpopints. At L'Eree, in front of the direction-finding tower, one of the few surviving networks of fire and communication trenches, linking concrete machine-gun positions and a 'Tobruk' pit which mounted a tank turret at ground level, have been opened up and can now be studied. There is no direct access to the adjacent direction finding tower.

UNRESTORED SITES

Underground Hospital. This is the largest tunnel network anywhere in the Channel Islands, comprising two linked underground complexes which housed the Guernsey Underground

Hospital in St Andrews. It was intended for the accomodation and treatment of wounded resulting from an Allied assault. Used briefly in 1944, it has been open to the public since 1954, but as yet has not been restored. Nearby parking.

Ammunition Tunnels. Lying in a wooded valley partly beneath the parish church of St Saviour, this German tunnel complex was built as one of several secure underground ammunition stores. Sections of the complex system remain in their incomplete state, showing the nature of the work undertaken

Unlike its 'twin' on Jersey, the Guernsey Underground Hospital has not been restored. Alec Forty

by the forced labourers under extremely harsh conditions. The concrete-lined entrance is open to the public and houses a display of military equipment. Parking nearby.

An example tunnel under St Saviours, whilst being photographed by Tomahawk Films. Brian Matthews

MUSEUMS

German Occupation Museum. This excellent museum, behind the Forest Church, near the airport, tells the story of the most dramatic five years in the island's recent history. Not only are there comprehensive military displays but also equal prominence is given to the civilian story, to tell the rigours of the islanders day-to-day life whilst under occupation. There are realistic tableaux and in the grounds are examples of the guns, vehicles and obstacles that were part of the extensive German defence works.

Parking, refreshments and WCs available.

One of the best and most comprehensive museums on the Occupation is located at Forest and contains a wealth of military and civilian memorablia as this photograph shows.
Author's collection

La Vallette Underground Military Museum. The tunnels at La Vallette have been converted into an award-winning military museum, which displays material relating to all periods of Guernsey's military history. The tunnels were designed to hold massive oil fuel storage tanks, one of which is preserved in situ, there is also a magnificent collection of memorablia belonging to the Royal Guernsey Militia, plus collections of German military equipment and vehicles.

HAZARDOUS SITES

Certain fortifications may contain hazardous areas, especially to young children. Nether the States of Guernsey nor the private owners of such properties can accept liability for any accident or injury to any person visiting these fortifications. Access is NOT permitted to certain of the sites shown on the map which are: the Direction Finding /Observation towers at Fort Saumarez, St Pierre du Bois, Castel and Vale Mill; HQ or Command Posts at Batterie Strasburg and 'Kernwerk'; Artillery Batterie Mirus and defence works there.

JERSEY – MAIN SITES OF INTEREST

CIOS Jersey list their eight most important fortifications of the Atlantic Wall in a leaflet (free), which can be obtained together with more information and opening times, etc, from their Hon Secretary at the address already given. The sites they list are as follows:

Underground Command Bunker, Noirmont Point, St Brelade. This impressive bunker extends down into the ground for 40 feet on two floors and was the Command Post for the coastal artillery battery located there. See up to date leaflet for opening times, admission charge and other details.

Coastal Artillery Observation Tower, Noirmont Point. A massive, most spectacular structure, perched on the clifftops. See up to date leaflet for more details.

10.5cm Coastal Defence Gun Casemate, La Corbiere, St Brelade. Adjacent to the road leading down to the lighthouse –

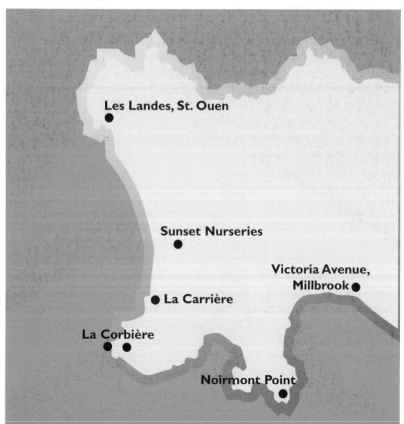

Les Landes, St. Ouen

Sunset Nurseries

Victoria Avenue, Millbrook

La Carrière

La Corbière

Noirmont Point

look for the signs. The bunker retains its original gun and many interesting relics. See latest leaflet for up to date opening times and admission charges. Take Bus Route 12, alight at the terminus and walk down the hill. There are toilets near bus terminus. Free car parking.

'M 19' Fortress Mortar Bunker with Tunnel System, La Corbiere. An interesting complex with an impressive tunnel linking it to a neighbouring bunker, it once housed a rare type of automatic mortar. It is situated on the right of the road leading down to the Lighthouse. See latest leaflet for opening times and facilities. Bus Route 12, alight at terminus and walk down the hill.

Coastal Defence Gun and Anti-Tank Casemates, La Carriere Point, St Ouen's Bay. A twin bunker complex adjacent to the Five Mile Road between La Pulente and Le Braye; it houses some of the larger relics including a railway truck, a tank turret and a searchlight. See latest leaflet for details. Bus Route 12A, alight at La Pulente and follow bus. Large car park.

Heavy Machine-Gun Turret Bunker at Val de la Mare, St Peter. With steel cupolas up to 10 feet thick, these bunkers once proliferated along the Atlantic Wall, now this is one of the few examples still left intact. Not on a bus route, but free car parking. See latest leaflet for more details.

Gun Emplacements and Underground Bunkers at Les Landes, St Ouen. A meticulously restored coastal artillery battery with many underground bunkers and lengthy passageways. Also on display is a 15.5cm coastal defence gun recovered from the foot of the cliffs in 1991. Bus Route 8 Alight at the Fine Gems and Crafts Centre. See latest leaflet for details of admission charges and opening hours, etc.

Anti-Tank Gun Casemate at Millbrook, opposite La Rue de Galet. This bunker is almost in its original condition and contains a rare, restored Czech 4.7cm anti-tank gun. On all bus routes to West of Island, alight at 'Benest's of Millbrook' and walk down La Rue de Galet. See latest leaflet for more details.

THE GERMAN UNDERGROUND HOSPITAL (GUH)

The largest and most spectacular 'time capsule' of the Occupation is the **Underground Hospital, St Lawrence,** which was dug out of the rock by large numbers of forced labourers, augmented by Russian POWs, who: '... toiled for twelve hours a day, like ants in an underground hell'. Since the 1960s the complex has been carefully restored, so that many areas are now

The unfinished tunnel.

Original layout of the Underground Hospital

1 Entrance (Meadowbank)
2A Electricity generator
2B Fuel store
3 Air locks
4 Reception store
5 Casualty assessment centre
6 Orderly's quarters
7 Kitchens
8-13 Wards
14 Collapsed corridor
15 Ward
16 Ward for senior officers
17 Dispensary/operating theatre
18 Operating theatre
19 Telephone exchange
20 Head storeman's quarter
21 Medical supply room
22 Medical storeroom
23 Air locks
24 Entrance (Cap Verde)
25 Lavatories
26 Boiler room
27 Escape shaft
27A Escape shaft
28 Unfinished tunnels
29 Corridors

The boiler room.

The operating theatre.

These illustrations are from the guidebook to The German Underground Hospital, Jersey, which now features their evocative 'Captive Island' exhibition. (Sanctuary Inns Ltd)

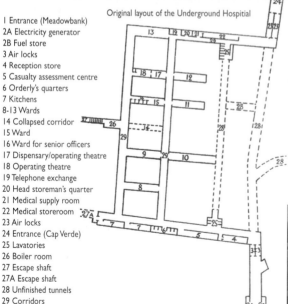

'fully functional'. In 2001 an entirely new state-of-the-art exhibition was opened, called: **'Captive Island'** which uses the latest electronic digital technology to tell the definitve story of the Occupation, taking visitors from 'Threatened Island', through to 'Daily Life', 'Resistance' and ultimately 'Liber-ation'.

This twin complex of coastal defence gun and anti-tank gun casemates are at La Carriere, St Ouen's Bay. Hawksworth

JERSEY MUSEUMS

In addition to the GUH there are four relevant museums, viz:

The Channel Islands Military Museum, St Ouen. Housed in a restored 10.5cm coastal casemate bunker is large collection of over 5,000 artifacts including an Enigma codemachine.

A heavy machine-gun turret bunker at Val de la Mare. Hawksworth

St Peter's Bunker Museum, St Peter. Housed in an underground bunker that was the HQ of MG Btl 16, with sleeping accomodation for 33 soldiers. Among the many relics is another Enigma code machine.

La Hougue Bie Museum, St Saviour. Several of the rooms in this restored battalion command bunker have been set up as reconstructions of their original wartime appearance. It is run by the jersey Museums Service.

Fully restored after being rescued from the bottom of nearby cliffs, this impressive 15.5cm K418(f) gun is on its turntable at Les Landes. Hawksworth

The Island Fortress Occupation Museum, St Helier. Located at 9, Esplanade, this is a converted warehouse and contains numerous WW2 relics, plus a miniature cinema showing occupation films.

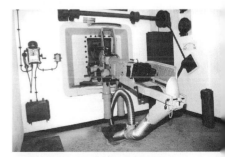

Fully restored with a wealth of detail is this anti-tank gun casemate at Millbrook, St Lawrence. Hawksworth

The Noirmont Point command bunker. This impressive bunker is on two floors and extends to a depth of 40 feet. Hawksworth

Also at Noirmont Point is this massive Coastal Artillery Observation Tower. Hawksworth

Adjacent to the road to the lighthouse at La Corbiere, St Brelade, is this 10.5cm casemate complete with its original gun. Hawksworth

Fortress Mortar bunker and tunnel system is also at La Corbiere. Hawksworth

THE OCCUPATION TAPESTRY

To celebrate the 50th anniversary of the liberation of Jersey, an Occupation Tapestry was created by the Jersey people. Its 12 panels tell the story of the Occupation years from the outbreak of war up to the liberation, including such detail as restrictions, everyday life, social life, civil government, deportations, escapes, etc. It is also run by the Jersey Museums Service.

ALDERNEY – MAIN SITES OF INTEREST

FORTIFICATIONS

Unlike Guernsey and Jersey, none of the fortifications have been restored. Indeed, at first glance there is little immediate visual evidence of all the hardware that was installed on this: 'battleship of concrete and steel anchored in front of the Atlantic Wall', as the German propaganda liked to describe it. The Ordnance Survey map of Alderney (Crown Copyright 1995) does show defences in some detail, so their locations are fairly easy to find and anyone interested can seek them out. However, the map does include the following warning:

'Exploring fortifications can be dangerous and should in no circumstances be undertaken without proper precautions and first obtaining permission where required. The States of Alderney cannot accept and liability for injuries to person, effects, or damage to property.'

186

Coastal Gun emplacement overlooking Clonque Bay. Martin Pocock

All that is left of the infamous SS camp at Sylt are the entrance pillars and concrete foundations. Martin Pocock

Also included on the OS map is much useful tourist information. Some of the larger, more obvious erections – such as the fire control tower (MP3) at Mannez Hill, Les Mouriaux Water Tower, Batterie Annes and the anti-tank wall at La Saline Bay, are shown in the accompanying photographs.

Alderney Society Museum.

Housed in a former schoolhouse, the collection covers the history of the island from prehistoric to modern times, so the wartime era is included. It should be remembered, however, that the island was almost completely evacuated of civilians and that, because of the use of slave labour (including Sylt Camp run by the SS), many of the German records have been destroyed.

SARK

Even the tiny island of Sark has its own small occupation museum

Notes

1. *Festung Guernsey* and its companion volume *Festung Jersey* are lavishly illustrated records of the German defences on the Channel Islands, which GenLt Graf von Schmettow caused to be produced, using the best artists and most skilled photographers of the *Divisionkartestelle* (Divisional Cartographic Section). The Guernsey set runs into four volumes, and contains an amazingly detailed record of the defences.

BIBLIOGRAPHY

Books

Aufsess, Baron von: *The von Aufsess Occupation Diary*, published by Phillimore & Co Ltd, 1985

Cameron, Norman & RH Stevens (Translators): *Hitler's Table Talk 1941-44 His Private Conversations* published by Weidenfeld & Nicolson, 1953

Churchill, Winston S: *The Second World War, Volume II - Their Finest Hour*, Cassell & Co Ltd, 1949

Coysh, Victor: *Swastika over Guernsey* Guernsey Publishing Co Ltd, 1955

Cruickshank, Charles: *The German Occupation of the Channel Islands*, Sutton Publishing, 1980

Dalmau, John: *Slave Worker*, The Guernsey Press Co Ltd

Durnford-Slater, Brig John: *Commando*, William Kimber & Co Ltd, 1953

Forty, George: *Channel Islands at War, a German perspective*, Ian Allan Publishing, 1999

Ginns, Michael, MBE: *The Organisation Todt and the Fortress Engineers in the Channel Islands*, CIOS Jersey, Archive Book No8, 1994

Grieken, Gilbert van: *Destination Gustav* The Guernsey Press Co Ltd, 1992

Hathaway, Dame Sibyl: *Dame of Sark – an autobiography*, Heinmann, 1961

King, Peter: *The Channel Islands War 1940-45* Robert Hale, 1991

Lamerton, Mark: *Liberated by Force 135*, ELSP in association with Nestegg Enterprises, 2000

Longmate, Norman: *If Britain had Fallen*, BBC, 1972

Mollett, Ralph: *Jersey Occupation Diary*, Seaflower Books, 1994

Sinel, Leslie: *Swastika over Jersey*, Guernsey Press Co Ltd, 1958

Speidel, Genlt Hans: *We Defended Normandy*, Herbert Jenkins, 1951

Warlimont, Walter: *Inside Hilter's Headquarters* Weidenfeld & Nicholson, 1964

Wilt, Professor Alan F: *The Atlantic Wall, Hitler's defenses in the West 1941-44* IOWA State, University Press, 1975

Books about German Bunkers

The following is a good selection of handy flexi-backed books about German fortifications on the islands:

a. Guernsey. *A Guide to German Fortifications in Guernsey* by Ernie Gavey, published by Guernsey Armouries, 1997

b. Jersey. *Jersey's German Bunkers* by Michael Ginns, MBE, (Archive Book No 9), published by CIOS Jersey, 1999

c. Alderney. *The Fortifications of Alderney* by Colin Partridge & Trevor Davenport, Alderney Publishers, 1993

Other CIOS Archive Books

No 1 - German M Class Minesweepers of the Channel Islands by John H Wallbridge

No 4 - German Armour in the Channel Islands edited by Peter J Bryans

No 5 - Merchant Shipping 1940-45 edited by Peter J Bryans

Railways in Guernsey by Frank E Wilson

CIOS Annual Review form 1973 onwards to date (back copies are available)

Operational Reports

BRITISH

Report on Operation DRYAD (No 5062 dated 9 Sep 42) by Maj G March-Phillips. SSRF

HQ Combined Operations Report (SR 1186/42 dated 19 Nov 42) on Operation BASALT by Maj JG

Appleyard, SSRF

Combined Operations Report (SR 1272/43) on Operation HUCKABACK

Office of Naval Officer in Charge, Channel Islands, Operation NESTEGG (No 0301/17 of 19 May 45)

GERMAN

319. ID report on Commando Raid on Sark 3/4 Oct 42. Abt.IaAz34gNo 431142 of 6 Oct 42

INDEX

Photographs are <u>underlined</u>

Hospitals, Underground, 122, 179, 184, <u>184</u>
Hunger Winter (*Die Grosse Hungerzeit*) - 42, 105, 125 et seq, 131 et seq

J

Jersey Occupation Map - 175

K

Kern, Lt - 37, <u>38</u>
King George VI - 19 et seq, 42, 144, 145
Koch - KptLt - 21, 37
Kriegsmarine - 53 et seq, 79, 97, 103 et seq, 105
   Artillerietraeger - <u>53</u>, 104, 135, *135*
   Coastal trawlers - <u>52</u>
   E-boats - 103
   Flak ship - 52
   Minesweepers - 103 et seq, <u>103</u>
   U-boats - 104, 125, <u>103</u>

L

Lanz, Maj Dr Albrecht - 11, 14, 21 et seq, <u>23</u>, 30 et seq, 34, 35, <u>39</u>, 41 et seq, <u>47</u>, 47, <u>57</u>, 139
Le Brocq, Norman - 134 et seq
Leitstande - 99 et seq
Liebe-Pieteritz, *Hptm* - 29 et seq
Lieutenant Governors - 14, 16, 18 et seq
Lindau, *Vizeadml* Eugen - 22, 30 et seq, 34
Luftwaffe - 23 et seq, 27, 31 et seq, 49 et seq,
Luftwaffe aircraft
   Do 17 - <u>50</u>, 53
   Fi 156 - 41, 53, <u>89</u>
   He 111 - 24, 69
   He 126 - 53
   Ju 52 - 30 et seq, <u>31</u>, <u>32</u>, <u>33</u>, 125
   Me 109 - <u>28</u>, <u>49</u>, <u>50</u>, 51,
   Me 110 - 32, 51

M

Maas, Maj Dr - <u>23</u>, 35, <u>39</u>, 44
Machine Gun Battalion 16 - 57, 58, 65, 85 et seq, 127
Maltzahn, Lt - 136 et seq
Marinenpeilstaende - 101, <u>101</u>, 102, 177, <u>177</u>
Mentha, Mr - 35
Merchant shipping - <u>104</u>, 105, 124
Militia - 19 et seq, 149
Mirus Batterie - 92 et seq, <u>93</u>, <u>94</u>, 108
Mueller, *Genlt* Erich - 56, 63 et seq
Museums - see Chapt 10
   Alderney Society - 187
   Channel Islands Military, Jy - 185
   German Occupation, Gy - 181
   Guernsey Museums and Art Galleries, Castle Cornet, Gy - 174
   Island Fortress Occupation, Jy - 185
   Jersey Museum Service, Elizabeth Castle, Jy - 174
   La Hougue Bie, Jy - 185
   La Vallette Underground, Gy - 181
   St Peter's Bunker, Jy - 185

N

Naval Direction and range finding towers - see *Marinenpeilstaende*
Naval Signal HQ - 105 et seq, <u>106</u>
'Nestegg' Operation - 139 et seq, <u>146</u>
Newspapers and their staff - 26, <u>78</u>
Nicolle Lt Hubert - <u>149</u> et seq

O

Obenhauf, *Ob Gefr* - 40

Observation Towers - see *Marinenpeilstaende*
Occupation Tapestry - 186
Occupying Forces - see Garrison (German)
Organization Todt (OT) - <u>67</u>, 68 et seq, 70 (crest), 72 (rank badges), 97, 109 et seq, <u>117</u>
Obernitz, *Hptm* von - 29 et seq, <u>38</u>

P

Palace Hotel , St Helier - 134
Pantcheff, Maj 'Bunny' - 109 et seq
Places to visit - 171 et seq (incl photos)
   Alderney - 186 et seq
   Guernsey - 175 et seq
   Jersey - 182 et seq
   Sark - 186 et seq
Plocher OTL - 37
Pope, George - 41
Porteous, Capt PA, VC - <u>167</u>
Power, Lt Col, HR - 143
POWs (German) - <u>147</u>, <u>148</u>

R

Raids on France (German from Channel Islands) - 135 et seq
Rationing - 77
Restored sites
   Guernsey - 176 et seq
   Jersey - 182 et seq
Royal Air Force - 6, 14, 88, 108, 149
RAF aircraft
   Avro Anson - 154
   Bristol Blenheim - 29
Red Cross 8, 127, <u>127</u>
Reicharbeitsdienst (RAD) - <u>61</u>
Richthofen, Gen Dr Ing von - 36
Robinson, Lt Col - 144, <u>144</u>
Rommel, FM Erwin - 7, 125
Royal Navy - 6, 14, 107 et seq, 123